FOR QUEEN AND CUMBERLAND

Martin Daley

First published 2008
Hayloft Publishing Ltd, Kirkby Stephen, Cumbria CA17 4DJ
Tel: +44 (0) 17683 42300   Fax: +44 (0) 17683 41568
Email: books@hayloft.euweb
www.hayloft.eu <http://www.hayloft.eu>

ISBN 1 904524 57 5

A catalogue record for this book is available from the British Library.

Papers used by Hayloft are natural, recyclable products made from wood
grown in sustainable forests. The manufacturing processes conform to the
environmental regulations of the country of origin.

For wee Charlotte

CONTENTS

LIST OF ILLUSTRATIONS

While I have tried to trace copyright holders for all illustrations featured in this book, I would like to apologise should there be any errors or omissions.

ACKNOWLEDGMENTS

Aside from the debt owed to the authors of countless primary and secondary sources, the list of those who contributed to this book through providing access to information, assisting in information gathering, or simply giving encouragement, is considerable. To them all, I express my sincere thanks, but special mention must be made of the following.

From a military point of view, the ever patient and accommodating Stuart Eastwood, curator of the Border and King's Own Royal Border Regiment Museum, deserves special mention for his support, enthusiasm, advice and his allowing access to and use of material belonging to the regiment. Stuart's opposite numbers, Captain (retired) Mick Holtby and Terry Brighton, at the Queen's Royal Lancers Museum, were equally as obliging, and the Royal Green Jackets Museum curator and regimental secretary kindly allowed the use of some superb illustrations. My researchers, P.A. Stanbridge and George Smith, provided sterling work and displayed their expertise in accessing individual records at the Public Records Office in Kew.

In terms of gaining access to civilian material, the list of assistants is a lengthy one: Carlisle historians Ashley Kendall and Jim Templeton; their counterparts in Penrith John Hurst and Colin Bardget; Richard Gaizely and Father Peter Chappell, who allowed access to St Catherine's School and Church records respectively; staff at the Carlisle Library, the Penrith Library, Penrith Museum and the County Records Office, to whom nothing was too much trouble; and family members Iris Kirk, Syd and Brian Scott and Muriel Ball, who all contributed vital anecdotal information that helped piece the various ancestral jigsaws together (much harder than your average 500-piece job, I assure you!)

The people who have directly contributed to producing this fine looking article itself are Dawn Robertson and the team at Hayloft, Lorna Reynolds, who edited, typeset and designed the cover (for quotes and enquiries contact lornareynolds@talktalk.net) and Dr Christophe Vever, skilled chiropractor and occasional proof reader, who read the entire manuscript and whose suggestions helped enormously. I thank them all.

Finally I must make special mention of my lovely wife, Wendy, whose patience and encouragement, when listening to me babble on about the causes of the Crimean War or the sanitary conditions in early 19th century Carlisle, never wavered. Cheers, chuck!

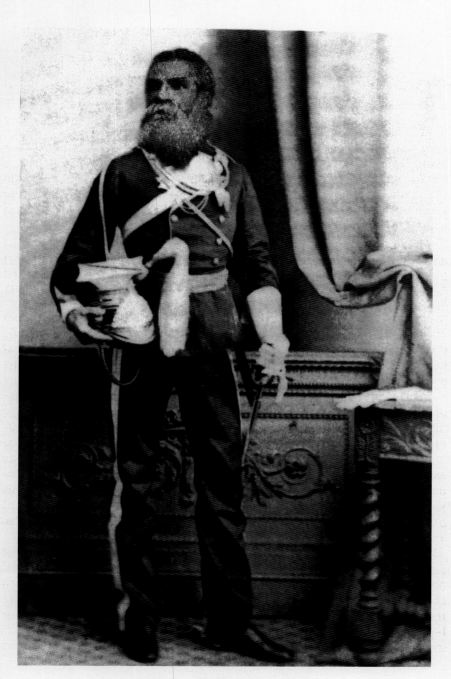

Private 1622 Isaac Scott of the 17th Lancers

INTRODUCTION

There are many who are prepared to champion the qualities and achievements of those historical heavyweights who are constantly drilled into our psyche: competitions to find the Greatest Briton, or a mad-rush campaign to canonise someone's favourite sportsman or pop star. As a result of this relentless modern-day media exposure, we know much about famous characters and their families; we could each probably have a decent stab at answering a few trivial pursuit questions about the Churchills, the Kennedys, or the Windsors. But how much do we know about our own family? From whom are we descended? Where is our place in history?

Presidents and Prime Ministers, Generals and Kings, all make the decisions that shape events, and lead them to the doors of the masses, but it is the people themselves who make history happen. Many of our own ancestors have taken part in some of history's greatest events and many have paid a devastating price for the privilege. It is they who, without ever meaning to, helped change the world, but sadly you won't see their names and faces in the history books alongside the great and the good. This book, the first in a series covering different periods in history, seeks to redress that imbalance by giving as much coverage to the ordinary as to the extraordinary.

Some family historians are happy simply to find out the name and dates of an ancestor and add them to a list: Joe Bloggs 1810-1870. But history for me isn't a museum or a collection of old documents, as interesting as they undoubtedly are; it is something that has flesh and blood. Surely old Joe is worth more than a scribbled date on a page? Who was he? What did he experience during his lifetime? What events, beyond his control, shaped his destiny and how did he react to them? The three main players in this volume all volunteered for service in the army, but for very different reasons; they are also all, through the lottery of births, marriages and deaths, ancestors of mine.

'Do you come from military family?' I was once casually asked whilst researching the army career of a forebear. My initial reaction was to say I did not; apart, that is, from my dad, who was a National Serviceman; and then of course, there were my grandfathers and great uncles, who all served in the Second World War; and not forgetting my great grandfathers and their brothers who served in the First World War. As the ancestor in question was my great (x2) grandfather, who had served in the Crimea and India in the

1850s, I realised I was answering one of those Pythonesque 'What have the Romans ever done for us?' type questions. This prompted me to do a little further digging afterwards, and it soon became apparent that my generation was in fact the first not to enter into military service in one form or another since the mid 18th century (so much for not coming from a military family).

There is, of course, nothing unique or even unusual about the fact that I am descended from generations of men in service. I would wager that every person reading this book would have similar ancestry, given the reduced population in centuries past and noting that the first subject of this book is my great (x3) grandfather and was therefore one of 32 great (x3) grandparents. Also, taking into account the population boom over the last century and a half—something that has turned family trees into ancestral forests—there is a sporting chance that any local readers may themselves be related to some of the men covered, however remotely. Whether related or not, I would encourage anyone to look into their own family history and learn about some of the figures from their own past.

We often boast about how advanced we are when compared with our forebears; we witness, and benefit from, more technological progression in one year than our grandparents did in decades. But can we claim to have had such adventures, witnessed such dangers, experienced such hardships, or contributed so much to our nation's development and security? If I ever did have a feeling of smug superiority over my ancestors, with my relative wealth of knowledge and comfortable lifestyle, I was soon taken down several pegs when I started delving into their way of life (perhaps existence is a better term) and discovering the sacrifices they made. In short, the stories of my elders and betters always leave me feeling extremely humble and insignificant by comparison.

Getting back to the book itself, perhaps it is worth taking a moment to point out what it is not. It is not intended to be a military epic; there are plenty of other masterly books of that genre on the shelves already without my attempting to add to them. Nor is it an effort to engage in some sort of sycophantic hero-worship, or exaggerate the military achievements of the men concerned, none of whom received promotion, were decorated, or were mentioned in despatches during their respective careers. These men, like the rest of us, were fallible in civilian life and were possibly guilty, whilst acting under orders, of what we would consider today to be atrocities during their military service.

The book is as much a social history as a military one, because to fully understand our ancestors—their ways, their attitudes—we must first understand the times and conditions in which they lived and worked; and as the development of Cumberland, and of Carlisle and Penrith in particular, are continuing themes throughout, it is also as much a local history as a family one.

It is no easy task to piece together the intrinsically linked series of events, prompted by some of history's most celebrated characters over decades, sometimes centuries, that influenced the destiny of these men, nor to interweave their ordinary lives with those of the extraordinary events and people of their day, especially when the men themselves kept no diaries or journals. Even when such complexity is realised the question then arises, where do you make the starting point of your story? The reigns of monarchs, the fighting of wars, the passing of centuries, are the usual marker points at which you can insert your historical stake; in family terms, the beginning of generations also suits the purpose, and this is the approach I have taken, giving a brief background to each man's family history before allowing him to take the lead role. The strategic positions on the battlefield and the national and international politics are interesting, and are hopefully covered sufficiently to give an overview of what was happening, but I am more interested in asking what was it like on the ground for the individual in the heat of battle or in their daily existence? In writing around the subject, blending fragments of records with family anecdotes and grand histories, I have attempted to provoke thought in you, the reader; putting you in their place, and asking you to decide what it must have been like.

The three supporting cast members I have invited to take centre-stage with the chief actors of history in this book are introduced in chronological order, with the underlying theme of this volume being the 19th century. This is a seminal period in British history, shaped by people who, at least for the latter two-thirds of the century, take their name from their queen who occupied the throne for the vast majority of her lifetime.

Like many, I am fascinated by the Victorians: the reform that took place; the generation of towns in the early period; the wonderful architecture; and the development of civic pride in its cities towards the end. From innovation to fashion, what is classic history to us was the height of modernity to them.

As this series of books progress, we meet painters and decorators, joiners and labourers, tailors and weavers, and I make no apology for stressing again: these were ordinary people. Staying with the three main men of this volume and using them as an example, I am fascinated by the almost absurd incongruity of their lives; the diversity of their experiences: the industrial revolution in Carlisle and the harsh climatic conditions of Russia; or the quiet market town of Penrith and the dangers and exotic locations of Africa and Asia. And yet, whether Carlisle or the Crimea,

Penrith or Pretoria, the constant fight, both literal and figurative, against death and disease remained unceasing. They didn't know it but these young men were pioneers and would become figures of inspiration.

Like all histories, mine is partial and no doubt some readers will disagree with my findings. It is a truism that history is riddled with ambiguities and half-truths that cause disagreement and furious quarrels amongst its most erudite of scholars. During the years of research that went into this book, I discovered countless eminent historians (and sometimes, even eye-witness accounts) who disagree on certain events; I am left concluding that none of us can ever be one hundred per cent sure about events that occurred in another time, in another place and in very different circumstances from those with which we are familiar today. Of course, there is truth somewhere in all the events that have happened in the past, but the greatest challenge that historians have is in finding the most credible route to discovering that truth. For my part, the best I can offer is the assurance that I have thoroughly researched the subjects covered. I am confident that there are no great howlers in the book, but if inaccuracies do occur, I take full responsibility and I console myself with the fact that those greater historians than I continue to disagree over versions of bygone events.

One last question must be covered: that of judging someone's character or actions. Whilst we can challenge each other's defamation today through the due legal process, it is easy to judge historical figures harshly from the comfort and relative security of our 21st century armchairs, especially given that they can offer no response when having their actions questioned. Any criticisms levelled at individuals and establishments throughout the book are thoughtful and considered. This book presents a very personal view of history. If I have not done my ancestors justice, don't look too unkindly on them; it is my fault, not theirs.

Martin Daley
Carlisle
June 2004

JACOB REED

Handloom Weaver & Private with the 2nd Battalion the Rifle Brigade

✳ ✳ **1** ✳ ✳

It would be hard to imagine a more oppressive start in life than that experienced by Jacob Reed. Born in 1817, in the desperately impoverished area of Caldewgate in Carlisle, his father David earned a pittance in a dwindling profession while his mother Jane scratched around for casual work to supplement her husband's meagre income. The city had a population of 12,000 at this time, 0.1 per cent of a country that was still coming to terms with the end of the Napoleonic Wars.

At the time of Jacob's birth the working class population in Carlisle was effectively divided into three: the first comprising general tradesmen such as joiners and shoemakers, the other two reliant on the textile industry, either scraping an existence as a handloom weaver or enjoying a slightly more tolerable life employed in one of the cotton factories. David Reed came in the middle category: one of 5,000 handloom weavers working in Caldewgate and the neighbouring wards of Shaddongate and Denton Holme.

The textile industry in Carlisle was approaching its centenary by this time, the first factory having opened in 1724. It was fifty years later, however, when laws were relaxed to allow purely cotton fabrics to be produced (until then, wool production had been favoured) that cotton manufacturing in the city really took off. The River Caldew provided hard water that was perfectly suited for bleaching and, to maximize the supply, dams were built for both the Corporation and Denton Home mill races, as newly-built factories sought to take advantage of the plentiful natural resource. The Forster and Ferguson families both started successful businesses, and as the latter's empire expanded during the early years of the nineteenth century, the Ferguson brothers invited their brother-in-law, Peter Dixon, to help out. By 1812, the whole Dixon family had moved to the city from West Cumberland. It would not be long before the Dixons would become an influential family in their own right. Peter Dixon would build his cotton factory in Shaddongate in 1836; it was the largest of its kind in the country and had a chimney of over 300 feet. The chimney continues to dominate the city's skyline today.

Carlisle Canal in the 1830s (Carlisle Library)

A watercourse was built through Denton Home and Shaddongate, flowing back into the river at Willow Holme, as businesses boomed. The factories spun and finished the cloth, while the weaving was done by hand loom, their operators working from home or in weaving sheds. The weavers would receive yarn from the factory, work the material, and take back the lengths of cloth. Vast quantities of cheap cotton fabrics—suitable for warm climates—were produced and exported, as Carlisle became the fourth most important cotton-producing area in Britain.

As the city gradually put itself on the industrial map, so improved communication links were required. The most imaginative around this time was the proposal to build a canal from the city to the Solway coast. Work began in 1819. A small hamlet east of Bowness called Fisher's Cross—11 / miles from a basin in Caldewgate—was renamed Port Carlisle. Four years and £90,000 later, the Carlisle Canal received its grand opening on 12th March 1823. The Ship Canal could take vessels of 80-100 tons, with the limit in size dictated by the eight locks, through which the larger ships could not pass. Timber, coal and lime were all imported into the city as a result.

But the Industrial Revolution was proving to be less than kind to the thousands of handloom weavers in Carlisle. With such growth in their trade came the demand for greater technology, and when the power loom was invented in the cotton industry in 1785 it signalled the death-knell for the handloomer. To add to his problems, in the twenty years since the invention the city had witnessed a significant growth in population, which in turn had brought an overabundance of labour to a profession that was already top-heavy with personnel. Handloom weaving was an easy trade to learn, requiring only one shilling per week to rent a loom, and was ideally suited to the Scots and Irish immigrants who poured into Carlisle in the early years of the century. As a result of the changing face of his industry, the weaver's pay had steadily fallen since the turn of the century from 15s per week to 8s per week and by the time of his son Jacob's birth, David Reed found himself effectively pauperised.

Reed compared poorly even with his journeyman cotton-worker counterpart who, admittedly, had to work 12–14 hours per day in the factory (these were hard times for everyone), but could earn more than twice the figure of the self-employed handloom weaver. Moreover, the health and well being of the factory worker was reasonably good when compared to the numerous handloom weavers who were crowded together in the ill ventilated weaving shops or sheds.

If working conditions for the Reeds were miserable, then living conditions were worse. As impoverished immigrants flocked to the already overcrowded Caldewgate, many of the confined lanes, yards and courts, that were once gardens attached to houses fronting the main streets, gradually changed from private dwellings into workshops, stables, taverns and outhouses. Soon every available space would be built upon and with such unplanned urban growth taking place before the advent of adequate sewerage and decent water supplies, disease and malnutrition were inevitable.

Even by the odoriferous standards of the day, the environment in which these people lived is — to us — unimaginable. Many of the house drains became choked up; human and animal faeces ("nuisances" to the delicate middle class reader of the day) would mix with stagnant water to form a congealed sludge that sat in channels in the decaying streets and alleys. A stream known to locals as 'the Beck' flowed lazily through the open street in Caldewgate, finally finding its way through the long dank, dark and dirty sewer into 'la'al Cawda' — the River Caldew. (This was all in addition to the open sewers that surrounded the city and emptied into the rivers). The lack

A handloom weaver in the early 19th century

of water and such defective construction of the drains—something for which there was no regulation—combined with the smells from the slaughterhouses that dotted the area, would result in a lingering potent stench that hung over the tightly knit claustrophobic lanes, courts and alleyways like a gloomy shadow.

The staple diet for the lower classes consisted mainly of potatoes, bread—made of barley and rye—and oatmeal made into scones or thick pottage (made from boiled oatmeal and water), which was eaten for breakfast or for supper. Meat was an unheard-of luxury. William Fairish was a contemporary of Jacob Reed, born in 1819, and also the son of a handloom weaver. In his autobiography written in 1889, he stated that he had never seen a joint of meat on his father's table, adding mournfully, "The cry of discontent and the wail of famishing women and helpless children could be heard in every street."

The city had already witnessed food riots in 1795 and 1812; now in 1817 desperation was such that discontent amongst the lower classes was leading to criminal activity: two weavers were transported for stealing bags of meal from a Caldewgate warehouse, whilst their two women confederates were sent to the House of Correction. In a separate incident another weaver was transported for seven years for stealing a piece of white calico. Ten years earlier, feeling secure in its newfound industrial wealth, Britain had abolished its trade in slaves, and yet here were her subjects scavenging like dogs. All the weavers had by way of support was their guild. The guilds were in effect the forerunners of the trade unions we know today. It was their task to ensure goods were kept up to a high standard of quality and in so doing protect the reputation of their members. A guild (there were eight in Carlisle) would also hold funds out of which members could help any of their colleagues who were sick or in trouble.

By this time so many of the weavers were in trouble financially that the guild itself was powerless to do anything. And it wasn't just the weavers: a year after Jacob's birth it was calculated that between half and two- thirds of the population of Carlisle was living in abject poverty. Instead of ploughing their resources into eradicating such injustice, the Tory oligarchs who ran the city instead employed spies and agent provocateurs, who roamed the deprived areas on the lookout for the rioters' ringleaders.

In truth, the workers did not want to break the law to get a fair deal. With a groundswell of support from the Celtic immigrants, such was the desperation of the weavers' guild, that they actually petitioned the Regent to send their members to British America, as they could not support their families. This was not exactly serfdom but the weavers were experiencing similar hardships and injustices. (This petition went unanswered, as did a similar one sent to the Home Secretary, Sir Robert Peel, in 1827).

Poverty-stricken areas of Carlisle such as Caldewgate were representative of many lower class areas throughout the country. The first two decades of the nineteenth century had seen a growth in manufacturing and an increase in the number of factories, due in no small part to the boom in the cotton industry. Mechanisation of textiles in Britain produced a huge demand for raw cotton from the burgeoning plantations throughout the southern states of America; plantations that were reliant on black slaves to satisfy such an increase in demand. Any illusion the masses had, however, of enjoying greater health, wealth and a feeling of influence in the post-war regeneration of Britain was proving to be just that: an illusion.

The existing, outmoded system of parliamentary representation meant that many urban centres that had grown rapidly during the early phases of the Industrial Revolution and had no Member of Parliament to support their interests. The two main parties of the day were the Tories and the Whigs (or, as they were known in Carlisle, the yellows and the blues respectively). It was the Whigs who took the extension of the right to vote, but it was the Tories who held most of the cards; they not only sat in central government but, significantly, held power in the majority of the 250 towns and cities around the country that had at one time or another received a

Glovers Row, Carlisle (M. E. Nutter) (Tullie House Museum & Art Gallery)

Royal Charter to have their own council or corporation. It was the corporations that fixed the local bye-laws and taxes and virtually controlled everything that happened in the city. And if you were a low-born nobody like David Reed, it was impossible to remove these oligarchs because they could not be voted out; only the members of the corporation themselves were allowed to vote. As a result, nepotism was rife as this small group continually re-elected themselves or brought friends and relatives on to the council, while ignoring matters like water supplies, drainage and street cleansing; all issues they were supposed to oversee.

Social unrest became endemic across the country as an unprecedented growth in population was compounded by the disbanding of large numbers of soldiers and sailors after the wars, while high food prices and widespread unemployment all contributed to a feeling of malcontent amongst the working populace. Political activists attempted to quicken the pace of Parliamentary reform by organising rallies with the aim of improving representation for the masses, which would in turn, they hoped, improve living and working conditions.

Both locally and nationally, there was agitation a-plenty. One flashpoint in particular shocked the nation. The Manchester Radical Union organised a meeting for 16th August 1819, at St Peter's Fields on the outskirts of the city, to call for political reform. Some 60,000 people gathered for the meeting, including many women and children. The main speaker at the meeting was to be Henry Hunt, a prominent radical orator, but the magistrates decided to arrest him before he could deliver his speech. This infamous event saw the Manchester and Salford Yeomanry (part-time cavalrymen) wading into the crowd to arrest Hunt. In so doing, the horsemen trampled a young girl to death, and they quickly found themselves surrounded by furious demonstrators. The scene degenerated still further and regular Hussars were sent in to rescue the part-time soldiers. When the dust settled and the panic subsided on what had been planned as a peaceful rally, eleven people lay dead, while four hundred more were seriously wounded. Peterloo thereafter became a byword for the popular perception of high-handed and tyrannical Tory rule. Moreover, it had a profound effect on 'Radicals' throughout the country. Two months after the Peterloo Massacre, the Caldewgate weavers held meetings and armed themselves with pikes before taking to the streets. Extra cannon were placed in the castle and more troops were drafted in.

As the 1820s wore on, the population of Carlisle expanded from 14,500 to 19,000. At the turn of the century, the highly respected (but largely ignored) archdeacon of the city, William Paley (1743-1805), had warned the authorities about future rebellion. Towards the end of his life he wrote prophetically, "The most frequent and desperate riots are those which break out amongst men of the same profession, [such] as weavers." His warnings went unheeded and twenty years after his death things were getting worse instead of better.

✳ ✳ 2 ✳ ✳

As we have seen, the streets of Carlisle were lined with something, but it certainly wasn't gold. This message however, was not getting through to the Irish immigrants, whose numbers to the city at around this time peaked, as did, unsurprisingly, the number of handloom weavers. Overcrowded Caldewgate, with its downtrodden, half-starved inhabitants, devoid of income and with poor living conditions that lacked sanitation, gradually degenerated into a no-go, lawless area. The lower classes who lived there were not necessarily inclined to revolution but, like their counterparts throughout the country, were forced to seek any way of protecting and enhancing their interests. In all the pages of Carlisle's history, the city had seen nothing quite like it.

And as if life wasn't cruel enough, in 1822 Mother Nature added her own spiteful potion to the mix. The *Carlisle Patriot* described the winter as 'remarkable for hurricanes and torrents of rain.' This all culminated in the flooding of the city on the night of 1st February 1822. The report of the flood by the *Patriot* gives a staggeringly familiar account of the incident to the Carlisle reader of 2005:

> *During Friday night a storm of wind came on from the South West and continued the whole of Saturday. At six in the morning the embankment which separates the race course from the terminus gave way, taking the greater number of inhabitants by surprise, catching many of them in their beds. By day the Eden had attained a great height; it was considerably higher than the great flood of 1771. In the alarm and confusion, several dragoons narrowly escaped drowning in their stables. One soldier swam back into the flooded building and dragged his horse out by its mane. The water reached the ceilings of the houses in low lying Rickergate. The Caldew was not greatly affected by the rain; but the back water from the Eden inundated the greater part of Caldewgate. Several brick buildings were destroyed and trees overturned; slates were lost in all directions while panes of glass shattered and chimneys were blown down.*

Was there any respite for these people? Leisure activities were a premium but venturing into the city did afford the opportunity of at least watching horse racing or the more gruesome 'sports' of bull baiting or cock fighting. Even this was not without its perils, however, as a closer look at one of these sports attests. Bull baiting involved tying a bull by its nose to a ring in the Market Place where it was attacked by packs of dogs. There was virtually no protection for spectators, and the frantic bull regularly broke free and veered into the crowd, causing injuries and even deaths. (Such blood sports were banned completely in 1835.) The more sedate activity of horseracing took place on the Swifts (hence the *Patriot*'s reference to the racecourse in relation to Rickergate).

As for the children, the working classes of areas such as Caldewgate and Shaddongate had other injustices to overcome: food was scarce, leisure activities were zero and education was haphazard at best. Some schools were provided by churches; others, like the well-meaning but inadequate Holme Head and Shaddongate Schools, were paid for by factory owners for the children of their employees. The young Jacob Reed, however, like many of his contemporaries, had to be satisfied with local men who ran short 'courses' in very basic reading in their own houses. Being forced into work at eight, however, Jacob gained little benefit from even this most basic of schooling.

His father, meanwhile, was interested in happenings elsewhere in the restive country and his like would demand a second opinion besides that of the local press. The London newspapers would arrive on the mail coaches to the city and usually fan the flames of insurgency amongst the Carlisle weavers. David Reed and his colleagues would eagerly await the coaches and retire to their weaving sheds in groups. Gathering round the fire, a nominated reader would go through the *Weekly Despatch*, *Bell's Life*, and the tri-weekly *Evening Mail* published by *The Times*, to inform his colleagues of the latest Reform meetings and national riots. The points would then be debated long into the night.

If the authorities did not realise the strength of feeling in such deprived wards, by 1826 they were soon about to. Things came to a head on Tuesday 6th June. The morning was pleasant and warm, but by sunset it would be marked down as one of the blackest days in the city's long and colourful history.

General Election campaigning was in full swing and the Tory candidate, Sir Philip Musgrave, was to pay that once-in-a-lifetime visit to Caldewgate to tell its inhabitants how great things were and how he was the man to lead them forward. This was mistake number one. At eleven o'clock Sir Philip entered a weaver's shop in Milburn Buildings. After debating the controversial Corn Laws and parliamentary reform with the sceptical yet well-informed weavers, Musgrave turned to leave and was confronted by scores of weavers clearly intent on making their point to their Member of Parliament. Sir Philip was forcibly given a lesson in the art of weaving, while his retinue were unceremoniously ducked in the mill dam. When a way clear for his party was made, they were pelted with stones and cobbles by the angry mob. Two of his colleagues scrambled their way over Caldew Bridge back into the city and alerted the mayor to what was happening.

Mistake number two came when Mayor William Hodgson, outraged by the situation, decided to gather a magistrate and the entire police force (two constables) and gamely march into Caldewgate to read the Riot Act. This was as ill-advised as Musgrave's visit: the mayor was abducted and the constables suffered the same fate as Sir Philip's followers. By one o'clock a 120-strong detachment of infantry troops (55th Regiment) was called out from the castle garrison and were ordered to fix bayonets and march over the bridge to disperse the crowd and rescue his worship. They were greeted with a shower of stones and missiles from a crowd of weavers that outnumbered them five to one.

High farce then turned to tragedy when the soldiers were ordered to open fire, supposedly above the heads of the crowd. One young woman, Mary Birrell, was said to have been watching the confrontation below in Queen Street from her first floor window. She was shot in the head and killed. (Reports of Mary's death were contradictory: some claimed it was an accident, while others reported her as being an agitator with stones found in her apron when her body was recovered.)

Others were wounded in the shooting but the saddest result of all came when a group of terrified children were huddled together in the middle of their Shaddongate School classroom by their teacher, who was attempting to protect them from the violence outside. During the shooting, one stray bullet smashed through the shuttered window of the classroom and hit 13-year-old Isabella Pattinson in the head. The little girl died later that night.

The unrest did not end there. Although the Mayor was rescued by the military, four days later he was set upon and so badly beaten that he received life-threatening injuries. These were dangerous times.

In an effort to control such seditious inclinations and civil disturbance, a committee of local Whig businessmen applied for the Police Act, and were elected as police commissioners with Home Office approval, much to the annoyance of the hitherto lackadaisical Tory-controlled Corporation. If the Tories had been shortsighted in their approach to appeasing the masses, then the Whig committee were to prove themselves heavy-handed; either way, the net result would be more of the same. By adopting the stick approach rather than that of the carrot, in 1827 they appointed Benjamin Batty as superintendent of their new force. Batty was from Manchester and was well versed in their no-nonsense approach to policing; but his straight-between-the-eyes tactics were soon to backfire.

Before his first visit to Caldewgate and Shaddongate, much like Sir Philip he had failed to properly gauge the depth of feeling amongst the inhabitants concerning their dire situation. The same hundreds-strong disgruntled crowd of weavers greeted him and as the visit progressed, the mood of the already restless throng turned increasingly ugly. Batty still failed to comprehend their mood and — whether through arrogance or ignorance (or a combination of both) — made one supercilious, throwaway comment too many. This sparked a firestorm of protest that saw the weavers again descend into all-out riot. The terrified police chief had to take refuge in a local shop and when his subordinates failed to secure his safe passage, the military were called in to disperse the crowd. This tactic had echoes of the Peterloo Massacre in 1819, something that would not have been lost on Batty, who had been present at the disaster. A military watch was thereafter placed over Caldewgate to guard against further disturbance.

Against these odds, in the Reed household finances had meanwhile taken a slight upturn. David himself was still earning his paltry 8s a week, but his wife, Jane, was now working in the factory, assisted by their nine-year-old son, Jacob. This effectively doubled the Reeds' income, but it was not without its dangers. There had been a Factory Act passed in 1802 that was entitled the Health and Morals of Apprentices Act, supposedly to protect children in the workplace. In reality, it had little impact and Jacob Reed found himself performing menial but dangerous work such as crawling under moving machinery to clean out cotton fluff.

As the 1830s dawned, there was an air of change in both the city and throughout the country. The Radical Movement, for so long ignored and derided, finally appeared to have some momentum. Richard Cobden and John Bright were the two leading Radical MPs who campaigned for Parliamentary Reform (they would each have streets named after them in Caldewgate) and finally, in June 1832, the groundbreaking Reform Act was passed. This extended the right to vote, almost tripling the electorate.

But sadly for the lower classes, the status quo of squalor and want remained and, in a cruel twist of irony, before the first post-reform elections could take place in the winter of 1832, the masses were to be crippled by a cholera epidemic. The disease travelled to Europe via the trade routes from India and ravaged the poor of Britain in the very year they hoped would see radical change and improvement to their way of life.

As this new seminal year began, 15-year-old Jacob Reed, now too big and too old to crawl under machines in the factory, was himself working as a handloom weaver. His income supplemented his father's wage and the Reeds found themselves straining their collective necks just above the poverty line. That was until the killer disease hit Carlisle. The first case was reported in John Street, Botchergate, in January 1832. The disease spread with spectacular swiftness, ravaging the poorer parts of city which were already riddled with ill health. The authorities were reduced to adopting the sombre practice of posting up the daily return of cases and deaths at the market cross. Of the 448 reported cases, 265 proved fatal: one fatality out of every 75 of the population. One of those victims was David Reed, Jacob's father, and any hope that the family had of gaining relative wealth and security died with him. In the *Carlisle Journal* in March 1832, the Weavers' Guild complained that the lack of meat in their diet was a cause of why so many of them succumbed. Their complaints fell on deaf ears.

David Reed was one of 31,000 of his class who were wiped out throughout Britain due to cholera in 1832, yet the authorities appeared intent on turning a blind eye to the catastrophe. The general view was summed up by the *Edinburgh Medical and Surgical Journal* which haughtily declared it would review no more books on the subject because of 'the multitude of books which have recently issued from the press on the subject of cholera, and our determination no longer to try the patience of our readers'.

Jacob was now the main breadwinner, and the pennies earned by his mother Jane as a labourer in the factory were just about keeping their heads above water and, more importantly, out of the workhouses that summoned the most destitute.

Further legislation was introduced through the Factory Act (1833), which was designed to protect those (especially children) working in the factories, and through the Municipal Corporations Act (1835), which sought to break the oligarchy's stranglehold on the local corporations by extending the vote, but life remained unimaginably cruel for the vast majority of Carlisle's citizens.

How did it ever come to this? The Speenhamland system had been introduced in 1795 and was designed as a minimum wage for the unskilled (3s per week for a single man and 1s 6d for each dependant). The system in reality had disastrous consequences as it encouraged employers to pay low wages, safe in the knowledge that the Speenhamland rates would pay the balance. With Jacob scratching just over 8s per week, he didn't qualify for such aid anyway. The system remained in force until the Poor Law of 1834 was introduced. This prohibited 'outdoor' relief for able-bodied men, who in future would only be financially assisted if they went into the workhouse.

St. Cuthbert's Workhouse (Ashley Kendall)

Paradoxically, it took money (and lots of it) to make the workhouses so horribly penal that even the most desperate would not want to surrender themselves to them.

There were three workhouses in Carlisle: St Mary's near Irish Gate Brow (1785); St Cuthbert's at Harraby Hill (1809); and, due to the unemployment amongst the Caldewgate handloom weavers in St Mary's parish, an additional Caldewgate workhouse which was built at Belle Vue in 1830. The able-bodied adults made ropes and broke stones for roads, while the old, infirm and children unravelled short pieces of old rope (oakum) and curled hair to make stuffing for mattresses. With more and more people being forced to move into the workhouses, twenty-six parishes around Carlisle came together to form a 'union'. Thus, the Board of Guardians appropriated St Mary's Workhouse for the reception of infirm paupers, St Cuthbert's was to be used for the able-bodied and Caldewgate for children.

In 1840 the recently formed Carlisle Mendacity Society discovered that over 300 people were destitute and entirely reliant on public charity. A quarter of the city's population were living on 3s or less per week, with (unsurprisingly) Caldewgate, Shaddongate and Botchergate containing the greatest concentration of poor. The death rate amongst Carlisle's adult population was now 6 per cent above the national average. The child (0-4) mortality rate was worse, much worse: a frighteningly high 50 per cent above the countrywide figure.

If Jacob thought that things couldn't possibly get any worse, they were just about to. Firstly, his mother died in 1842 in their squalid, rat-infested dwelling and secondly, in what was to prove the worst year for weavers' wages, his pay dropped below 7s per week. Jacob had escaped the workhouse by the skin of his teeth in 1832 when his father died; now, with his mother gone and the weaver's wage at an all time low, its gnarled claws were beckoning him once more.

The only glimmer of light appeared when the penny finally dropped amongst the city's hard-pressed authorities. The Carlisle Sanitary Association, formed in 1831 by a group of volunteers appalled by the apathy of the corporation, became alarmed by the increasing death rate and carried out an inspection of the city. Their subsequent report spells out in the most graphic terms the conditions in which Jacob and his lower-class contemporaries existed. They cut directly to the chase in their introduction:

> *Before entering upon the details of the inquiries made in each ward, the committee feel bound to express their extreme regret that Carlisle should present so much filth, and so much nuisances of the worst kind.*

It went on to describe the Caldewgate ward:

> *The lanes and courts are in a most objectionable state, containing almost invariably pigsties, open privies, dunghills, stagnant pools, the receptacles of every kind of filth; all of which nuisances remain unheeded for weeks and months together. Caldcoats presents dilapidated premises, numerous pigsties and disgusting necessaries.*

With half of Carlisle's God-forsaken souls living on the razor's edge between survival and starvation, another quarter could only continue with a struggle. After years of the authorities umming and ahhing, inspecting and deliberating, debating and considering, it was finally recommended that the Public Health Act should be applied to the whole of Carlisle.

Could the 1840s have been different for Jacob if the authorities had acted earlier? Perhaps early-century regulation of immigrants might have given him a better chance in life. And what about the question of education — something of which he had seen little: would greater access to learning have improved his opportunities?

This was no time for ifs, buts and maybes; the time called for action and the 25-year-old handloom weaver decided to leave the disease-ridden existence of civilian life and take the only other expedient available to him: that of joining the army.

Baggage waggons approaching Carlisle (Sam Bough, 1849)
(Tullie House Museum & Art Gallery)

✳✳ 3 ✳✳

In the eighteenth and nineteenth centuries, recruiting parties from regiments in the British Army would tour the country scouring areas (usually the local taverns) for new recruits. Their job was made easier during the 1840s as young men from the urban working classes like Jacob Reed were virtually beating down the doors of every military establishment in order to enlist and escape the clutches of civilian hardship.

The army at this time consisted of a hundred regular infantry regiments (numbered 1-99, plus the Rifle Brigade). In an effort to resolve the constant dilemma of how to spread the thin military resources between home and abroad, a trial expansion scheme was introduced in 1842 that saw nine regiments selected to form 'Reserve Battalions' from their depots. The Rifle Brigade was one of the nine and this is the regiment into which the young handloom weaver found his way. By the time Jacob enlisted in 1842, the Rifles had seen little action since the Napoleonic Wars.

No sooner had the young Carlisle man joined his new unit than he found himself travelling with them to their new barracks in Winchester; that is 'new' as in a change of venue as opposed to brand new facilities. The unhygienic conditions of civilian life stood Jacob in good stead for the barrack-room existence of the nineteenth-century soldier: conditions were foul. Men slept, ate and, well, did everything else in their barrack room. Lacking plumbing and sanitation, the barrack rooms were provided with a large wooden tub which had a dual purpose: washbasin by day, urinal by night. Consequently, the barrack-room stench was extraordinary. If you were the duty sergeant charged with rousing the men each morning, upon opening the door of the barrack room you were hardly greeted with a sweet aromatic waft of herbs and spices. Instead, the commingled stench of clay-pipe smoke, damp clothing, lamp-oil, the urine-tub, sour breath and unwashed feet was the nineteenth century potpourri of the military dwelling.

The men received three meals a day. Breakfast consisted of bread and tea, while lunch would be meat (meat!) and potatoes, sometimes cooked separately, sometimes together as a stew. The third meal (or 'tea meal', taken at 5.00pm) was introduced in the 1840s but was rarely substantial, and Jacob and his colleagues soon adopted the habit of going into town to buy something extra from the 'hawkers', usually ex-soldiers themselves, who scratched around for a living.

Pay differed not only between ranks but also between arms of the

The Rifle Brigade in the 19th century (Royal Green Jackets Museum)

service too; for example, guardsmen and cavalrymen received more than infantrymen. Still, Reed found himself being paid a shilling a day (6d was deducted for subsistence, regulation uniform and medical treatment) with board and lodgings. One thing is for sure - Jacob Reed had never had it so good.

The weapon issued to the men was the Baker Rifle. Jacob's uniform of green jacket and black buttons was intended to make him as inconspicuous as possible. He carried a powder horn, a bag of bullets, his rifle and little else. The Rifleman was a light infantryman in every sense of the word and when he wasn't performing reconnaissance or skirmishing in ones and twos, the job of his unit was to lead off an assault on the enemy and to mop up afterwards.

Hardships were a given in Victorian times, whether in civilian life or in the military, and Jacob could have done a lot worse than the Rifle Brigade. The founders of the regiment introduced a Regimental School and Library. Private soldiers were encouraged to take advantage of the reading, writing and basic arithmetic that was offered to them. This was of particular benefit to Jacob who had received only the basics in education to date. Recruits would also receive lectures on military subjects and tactical and skirmishing techniques.

Particular attention was naturally paid to developing accurate shooting. The Rifleman's training day would be three parts shooting, two parts simulated skirmishing, one part light drilling. He would spend hours shooting at still and moving targets, perfecting his accuracy with the standard weapon. Riflemen were divided into three classes: bad shots, tolerably good shots and skilled marksmen. It was intended by the end of training that the latter category was full. One commentator summed up the Riflemen when he wrote, "The Rifle Brigade are skirmishers in every sense of the word; a sort of wild sportsmen, up to every description of fun and good humour."

On the wider European stage at this time, the peace that had lasted in Europe since Waterloo was finally disintegrating. France, Italy, Austria, Hungary and Germany would all witness either unrest or outright rebellion during the revolutionary year of 1848. Only the British and, significantly, the Russian governments did not fall. Significant, because the eternal 'Eastern Question' remained: what would happen to the foundering Ottoman (or Turkish) Empire? And more significantly still, given Russia's perpetual desire to take over Turkish seaways, what would the giant superpower's next move be in relation to it?

But these global shenanigans were not the concern of Private 3519 Jacob

Reed. He was instead preparing for his first overseas posting as part of the 2nd Battalion of Riflemen; he was destined for Canada, which was still a British colony at the time. The posting for English troops was always considered a decent one, and that's the way it was to prove for Private Reed. Sailing from Portsmouth to Nova Scotia, Reed repeated the journey his colleagues had made in 1842, when they were accompanied by the novelist Charles Dickens, who was on his way to Boston. A nonplussed Dickens later described his first sight of Halifax Harbour: "I suppose this Halifax would have appeared an Elysium, though it had been a curiosity of ugly dullness" (he perked up afterwards) "but I carried away with me a most pleasant impression of the town and its inhabitants, and have preserved it to this hour."

On Reed's transatlantic crossing in late 1847 was another Cumbrian who had recently joined the Rifle Brigade. John Ross was born in Stonehouse near Brampton on 18th March 1829. He joined the Rifles as 2nd Lieutenant in April 1846. Unlike Ross, Reed certainly wasn't aiming on a career in the army that would bring promotion, wealth and status; that was virtually impossible for the likes of him. An officer's commission was proof of gentlemanly status and military authority; a buyable commodity to the (often dim-witted) upper class few, but an impossible aspiration to most lower class others. (The notion that an individual could progress this way and command a body of men in battle seems wholly bizarre to us but it would be 1871 before the system was finally abolished.) John Ross would have paid around £450 for his commission.

Private Reed enjoyed a peaceful, largely uneventful four years in Canada. In fact, the first ten years of Jacob's service had been relatively comfortable; at times, even mundane. He must have been thankful that his hard civilian life was now far behind him. He was travelling and experiencing new cultures, educating himself into the bargain and getting paid for it. As far as he was concerned, there were no clouds on the horizon that could possibly spoil his view of the future. He could never have envisaged the roller-coaster existence he was to experience during the following ten years: encountering world famous characters; experiencing Mother Nature in all her viciousness; and, most extraordinarily of all, witnessing at first hand, man's inhumanity to man.

Private Reed returned to England with his 2nd Battalion in 1852. Their arrival coincided with the unexpected death of the army's Commander-in-Chief, the Duke of Wellington, on 14th September. Jacob's journey from his squalid upbringing was complete, when, resplendent in his immaculate green uniform, he marched with his colleagues at the head of the Duke's funeral procession, through the thronged London streets from Horse Guards to St Paul's on the morning of 17th November 1852. Could this ordinary semi-literate lad from Carlisle ever have imagined he would be involved in such pageantry?

But things were soon about to change. A few months after his finest hour to date, Jacob was to find himself preparing for action at the sharp end of Victorian soldiering. It was in early 1853 that an unlikely flashpoint occurred in the Holy Land that would lead to a full-scale war between Russia and the allied forces of Great Britain, France, Turkey and Sardinia.

Russia had long coveted access to the Ottoman Empire's Dardanelle Straits. Success in gaining a right of entry would allow traffic from her Black Sea ports to travel, unmolested, into the Mediterranean; such access could potentially destabilise Eastern Europe in the process. The gluttonously expansionist Tsar, Nicholas I (1796-1855), decided to force the issue in 1853. In January, the Tsar demanded Orthodox rights in the holy places of Turkish-ruled Palestine, following bloody clashes between Greek Orthodox monks, supported by Russia, and Roman Catholic monks, supported by France. Several Orthodox monks were killed and the Tsar claimed that the Turkish police had deliberately allowed them to be murdered. This was the reason he used for threatening to invade Turkish territory.

His intentions, and the whole Eastern Question, made Britain and France extremely nervous as they could see their own interests in the Middle and Far East threatened. The British ambassador to Constantinople tried to broker a settlement between Russia and Turkey, but by 1st July 1853 Russia was occupying Turkey's European principalities. France found itself becoming an uncomfortable bedfellow with its perennial enemy Britain in attempting to arrange a compromise, but this proved futile. On 4th October, confident of British and French support, the Ottoman Empire declared war against Russia.

The British press were horrified when, on 30th November, the Russian fleet surprised a poorly-armed Turkish force sheltering in the harbour of Sinope, on the northern coast of Asia Minor. Five thousand Turkish sailors were killed. News of the atrocity reached Britain on 12th December and served as the catalyst for the entry of Britain and France into the war. The *Carlisle Patriot* reported the grim news:

> *Due to the Tsar's belligerence, Britain could be dragged into a war, whose cause we know very little about. Our army is gathering and unless there is a marked changed in attitude, a conflict, on a scale not seen since Waterloo, will be upon us.*

The words of the *Patriot's* editor were to prove both profound and

The Russian and Ottoman Empires

alarmingly accurate, as men from both local regiments, the 34th
Cumberland and 55th Westmorland (they would both join together in 1881
to form the Border Regiment), were to take part in the campaign and form
part of the largest foreign taskforce to leave British shores in sixty years.

Another of Carlisle's finest, Private Jacob Reed, set out from Portsmouth
with the Rifle Brigade in January 1854 aboard *The Golden Fleece*. By the time
they arrived in Malta in early March, war already looked inevitable. The
previous week, a joint ultimatum had been sent to Tsar Nicholas: unless
Russian troops withdrew from Turkey's European states by the end of April,
war would be declared.

The arrogant Nicholas ignored the warning, as if to call the Allied bluff.
It was a gross misjudgement: despite uncomfortable Anglo-French relations,
France and Britain declared war on 27th and 28th March respectively. The
misjudgements made by the Tsar were to cost the lives of half a million of
his own subjects.

✳ ✳ 4 ✳ ✳

On board with Jacob, as their ship pulled out of Valetta Harbour on 20th March, were three men who would provide a fascinating insight into the forthcoming campaign. The first two were members of Jacob's regiment themselves: Private Harry Blishen was a young man who, like the thousands of others, had been roused to join the army during the previous winter after hearing tales of adventure and glory. (When read dispassionately, his letters home to his mother could have been written by any young man during any war.) The second man was Captain Henry Clifford, who would not only keep a diary of his experiences but who would provide a stunning collection of watercolour paintings that would vividly express the horrors and hardships of war. The third person, who would distinguish himself with his reports from the front, was a little-known Irish journalist sent out by *The Times* newspaper to cover the war. Perhaps unknowingly, William Howard Russell was to carve himself out a reputation as the first (and still one of the best) war correspondents. He would become the doyen of his profession, both thrilling and shocking the nation with his reports for *The Times* and the *Daily Telegraph* from all corners of the globe over the following forty years.

As war was declared, the question of their Christian nation allying itself to Muslims was certainly confusing to the British people, as were the obscure objectives of the war, but that did not deter hundreds of young men like Harry Blishen flocking to recruit, intoxicated by reflections in the press about great victories at Trafalgar, the Peninsula and Waterloo. They did not know what they were letting themselves in for; many would not return to their homeland, as it was not only the Russians who were to suffer.

The Crimean War signalled the end of the 'Long Peace', as it was Britain's first major military action since 1815 when Wellington led British forces against the French. Because of such lengthy inactivity, successive governments had cut down on military expenditure, so the troops being shipped out to the Crimean peninsula had relatively poor equipment and virtually no experience of a foreign military campaign. (Although a handful of officers were veterans of the battle against Napoleon at Waterloo, they were now in their sixties and seventies and had to be constantly reminded that they were now allies of the French!)

On Wednesday 5th April *The Golden Fleece* anchored at a place unheard of in 1854 but one that would create its own horrific passage in history some sixty-one years later: Gallipoli. There they remained until, in early September, they joined a force of 50,000 Allied troops and sailed to the

Crimea via Varna (now Bulgaria).

In blazing, unhygienic Varna the taskforce encountered that old Victorian killer: ten thousand men were lost to cholera before they even set foot on the Crimea. The cholera-weakened, dispirited survivors, wracked with dysentery for good measure, finally landed on the western coast of the Crimean peninsula some 35 miles north of Sevastopol on 13th September 1854 at the ominously named Kalamita Bay.

The following day British officers immediately demonstrated their ineptitude and lack of organisation as they tried to get their men on to the beaches. By the time they set foot on enemy sand, their French counterparts had pickets four miles inland. (Fortunately the Allied landings were unopposed). The army's first night ashore would serve as an ill-omened prelude to the mismanagement that was to dog the whole campaign. William Howard Russell wrote in one of his first despatches:

> *Few will forget the night of the 14 September 1854. Seldom or never were 27,000 Englishmen more miserable. No tents had been sent ashore and the night closed in; the wind rose and the rain fell in torrents. The men were soaked through their great coats and blankets.*

The French and the British were now in theatre as one allied army, and it didn't take long for those among the rank and file to note the different methods adopted by the respective officers. The French were promoted on merit, while the British had the purchase system (the system that saw the wealthy buy their way through the ranks). The French therefore had the confidence of their men, while their British counterparts compensated for their immaturity and inexperience by continually barking out meaningless orders to their already bedraggled men. One of Jacob's fellow Riflemen, Private Harry Blishen complained in a letter home:

> *We were drilled incessantly upon our arrival, almost harassed to death and I am sorry to say we lost several men through the effect. We were drilled to give the young generals an insight of what they would have to do on the battlefield. Instead of being drilled at home, or kept in an efficient state of discipline, which they ought to be, they are sent out here to reduce the strength of our army, and to render men unfit to fight when they are called upon.*

Harry, Jacob and their colleagues did have some relief and acknowledgement of their efforts when they were visited and inspected by Omar Pasha, the commander-in-chief of the Turkish army on Saturday 16th September. Pasha was particularly impressed with the green-jacketed riflemen as they dashed passed him in double time. He rewarded them with an extra ration of rum.

Within a week of their arrival, the allies set off on their march towards Sevastopol, safe in the knowledge that if they could secure control of this key city and defeat the massed Russian army within, then ultimate victory would be theirs. This fact was not lost on the Russians either, and after their intelligence had reported the allied landing they sent out an army from the city to confront the enemy. Prince Mentschikoff led an army of 36,000 Russian infantry, 3,400 cavalry and 2,500 artillerymen with 122 guns and made his stance in a commanding position on a stretch of heights overlooking the River Alma. The plan was that the Prince would hold the Allies while Sevastopol fortified itself. So confident were the Russians of an easy victory that many of the city's fashionable set arrived as war spectators, with picnic blankets and opera glasses, in order to watch the spectacular unfold.

Marching south, the British soldiers adopted as their marching theme *Cheer Boys Cheer*, much in the same way their grandsons would march along to *It's a Long Way to Tipperary*, some sixty years later.

Private Reed saw his first taste of action on 19th September when the Rifle Brigade encountered the enemy at the River Bouljanak. This would simply be a precursor, however, to the main event the following day at the larger River Alma some six miles to the south.

The men marched and sang. Was their cheery demeanour just a bluff or a brave face? Each man, alone with his own thoughts, prepared for battle in his own way. One soldier wrote, "I felt horribly sick and a cold shivering ran through my veins." Captain Henry Clifford of the Rifle Brigade was a Roman Catholic and he wrote to his cousin afterwards that during the Alma, "I said my prayers the whole time and I received absolution just before going into battle." (Other, less devout, soldiers resorted to alcohol to numb the senses and bring on a kind of pre-battle narcosis. I for one don't blame them for that!)

Finally on 20th September the two sides came face to face. The 'Long Peace' was finally over as the first battle between major European powers since Waterloo, forty years earlier, was about to begin. Not only was the Russian army numerically stronger than the combined Anglo-French army, it occupied a position of immense natural strength with a redoubt erected behind its front lines. In theory, the Russians should have delivered the relatively easy victory they were anticipating. But battles and wars are rarely theoretical.

At six in the morning the French Zouaves (the equivalent of the Rifle Brigade) and Private Reed and his colleagues in the four companies of the

2nd Battalion, were called forward to lead off the attack. When Jacob formed up with his Company he saw the mammoth task that confronted them. They were standing on the northern bank, which sloped gently down to the water. On the opposite side were steep bluffs, 350 feet high. In order to take the Russian positions, the Riflemen had to wade through the water (shallow in parts, deeper in others) whilst laying down heavy fire to distract and draw the enemy, while their own artillery bombarded Russian positions; these two tactics combined would allow the line infantry regiments to pour across the river to confront the foe.

From the relative safety of the riverbank the men could see powder puff clouds of smoke popping out from the Russian batteries and tiny white spots of musket fire that preceded a faint distant snap. When the order was given for the Anglo-French Riflemen to advance into the water, however, what had almost seemed like harmless distant firecrackers turned into intense, murderous enemy fire, as the Russian showered their vulnerable attackers with all they could muster. Along with Jacob, Private Harry Blishen waded into the water that morning. He wrote to his mother afterwards, "We shot and made dreadful havoc amongst them." But such encounters are rarely one-sided, and Harry continued, "I am sorry to say that our poor fellows fell like grass before a scythe."

A pre-requisite of the Rifleman is his ability to fire, stop, re-load and fire again, almost in one cyclical movement. This was displayed perfectly as the Jacob Reeds and the Harry Blishens of the Rifle Brigade skirmished their way up the muddy incline. Private Blishen continued,
"While you are headlong in advance you had no time to be afraid - you don't worry so much when it's happening. If you hear a bullet whistling past you, you know you're all right."

The way the Riflemen conducted themselves appears to support the theory that once the action is under way, a soldier's training automatically kicks in and pre-battle fear turns to exhilaration and determination. Heavy artillery whistled and cracked overhead, bombarding the enemy positions, while the British redcoats joined their green-jacketed comrades on the steep southern slopes. Such was their position and their inability to organise themselves into their original units under such circumstances, the whole army virtually adopted a mass skirmishing offensive.

Once Private Reed (the infantryman) fired a shot, his weapon, charged with black powder, belched out a cloud of smoke, almost choking him in the process. The smoke became so dense on the southern bluffs, the British simply fired blindly into it. Continuous roar from cannon and small arms; voices of men on both sides shouting and shrieking in their death agony;

Fording the Alma (Lewis H. Johns) (Royal Green Jackets Museum)

attackers splashing through water and scrambling up the steep slopes; terrified defenders trying to drive them back into the water and out of harm's way. This wasn't some duel of grand strategy, too often depicted by many military historians: this was warfare at its most brutal, a claustrophobic groping in the dark, the winner of which was usually the side which held its nerve, rode its luck, and managed to make the best of this dangerous and confusing world.

On this occasion, that winner would prove to be the Allies. Despite the strong Russian position and their successes in driving the Allies back down the slopes on more than one occasion during the morning, the Anglo-French force would not be denied and attacks on the redoubt were soon in full flow by early afternoon. By four o'clock, after a full day of attack and counterattack, with Russians and Allies taking and re-taking the key Russian position, the allied army made their final advance. Yelling, smoke-blackened infantrymen, soaked in their own grimy sweat, clambered over their fallen colleagues, and surged towards the Russian positions to wreak havoc amongst the enemy. Seeing the British advance, the Russians turned and fled. The victory was complete. The Russians had lost, in a few hours, a position they thought would be held for weeks. The battle took one day to fight; the clearing up operation, collecting the wounded and burying the dead, took twice as long.

Lord Raglan, Commander-in-Chief of the British Army in the Crimea, wrote in his despatch, "The capture of the redoubt was materially aided by the advance of the four Companies of the Rifle Brigade, under Major Norcott." For his gallantry, Jacob's lieutenant, John Knox, was awarded the Victoria Cross.

One legacy of the Allies' first victory was a garbled report (not from Russell) that found its way into *The Times* on 2 October: *The Fall of Sevastopol* was the headline, and this filtered into the Carlisle press who, quite rightly, emphasised the efforts of the local regiment in the battle. (Alma would be awarded as a battle honour for the local regiment and one of the buildings in Carlisle Castle, along with other buildings named after battle honours, would, in time, carry its name.) Such optimism in the press, however, would prove to be not only inaccurate but also premature — almost twelve months premature in fact.

After Alma, had the Allies launched a further attack on the stronghold of Sevastopol when the Russians were both depleted and demoralised, perhaps the war would have been over almost before it had begun. The British and French command could not agree on such a strategy, however, and as a result the Alma would prove to be the first of a quartet of major, bloody battles.

It was not only the strategy on the battlefield that was interesting William Howard Russell by now. His concern for the health and wellbeing of the rank and file was regularly being emphasised in his reports. Supplies were lamentable; the colour of the coffee Jacob was drinking matched his jacket and Russell stated that the men only had two biscuits each between Alma (20th September) and 10th October. "Out of 35,600 men borne on the strength of the army, on 25 October there were no more than 16,500 rank and file," he wrote.

This date (25 October) was significant because of the infamous Battle of Balaclava, a battle during which the famous Charge of the Light Brigade took place. Jacob and his Rifle Brigade were to take no part in this particular cock-up. Ten days later, however, on 5 November, he would be involved in another battle where casualties on both sides would be horrific.

The Russian headquarters were in the ruined hill town of Inkerman. Below were a series of ravines and gullies that separated them from the British camp, directly opposite on a place called Home Ridge. The Russians planned to attack the British and drive them back towards the sea. Taking the Allies' lead from Alma, they attacked at dawn, catching the British by surprise; surprise that was compounded by thick fog that shrouded the heights. The Allies took heavy casualties and reinforcements were hastily ordered forward from Balaclava below. The first reinforcements were the Riflemen with General Pennefather's order, "Whenever you see a head, hit it," ringing in their ears. The Rifle Brigade reached the destroyed Home Ridge camp and Captain Henry Clifford wrote of seeing a large group of Russians emerging from the fog only fifteen yards away. He ordered the Riflemen to fix swords and charge at the enemy. Fierce hand-to-hand fighting ensued and Clifford later wrote of his men, "My brave lads dashed in amongst the astonished Russians bayoneting them in every direction." (Clifford was doing himself down a little here: he won a Victoria Cross for his own bravery at Inkerman!)

In the dreadful weather, the battle degenerated into pockets of disorganised skirmishes; the men did not know what was happening elsewhere on the battlefield because of the lack of visibility. Private Reed and the 2nd Battalion were called forward to support Captain Clifford and their 1st Battalion colleagues, fighting at close quarters with the enemy around the Home Ridge camp for most of the morning until they drove the Russians back. At twelve thirty, the disorganised Russians retreated in chaos.

Inkerman was a strange battle in many ways, not least that there was virtually no command structure due to the adverse weather conditions during which it was fought: the fog blotted out all view. It lasted for eight hours, starting with separately-fought infantry and artillery combats before slowly descending into a chaotic every-man-for-himself survival contest. One officer summed it up afterwards by saying, "Once engaged with the enemy, every man was his own General." (Strict discipline permeated the armies of the age for this very reason; for an individual's failure might swell into a collective panic.)

When the fog lifted, the true horror of what had occurred became known. Over two thousand men lay dead. The French General Bosquet described the Home Ridge camp as an 'abattoir,' while Russell, the *Times* war correspondent, described Inkerman as 'the bloodiest struggle every witnessed since war cursed the earth'.

Surviving two major battles and avoiding the disease that ravaged the army had been quite an achievement for the 37-year-old man from Carlisle. Through tremendous bravery and sheer good fortune, he and those of his colleagues who had survived the carnage dug in, preparing for the final advance on Sevastopol, the Russian stronghold that had received its first bombardment on 19 October. The main duties of the Riflemen consisted of being on the front line (as usual) and giving covering fire to the sappers and miners who dug the trenches in which, once they were completed, Private Reed and his colleagues would make their home.

Back in England the press coverage of the war, both nationally and locally, was reaching fever pitch. Carlisle's two main papers, the *Patriot* and the *Journal,* carried copies of Lord Raglan's despatches. The latest reports from William Howard Russell were printed, and seemingly endless lists of casualties would be documented on a weekly basis.

If the British thought the Crimean battles were bad, worse was to come. Barely a week after Inkerman, on the morning of 14th November 1854, the Rifle Brigade woke up in their tented camp to be greeted by rain and squalls. As the day progressed the weather deteriorated into a howling gale. By six o'clock in the evening it was a raging hurricane, speeding along at 100 miles an hour, ripping up the lightweight summer tents of the British. Russell wrote, "The air was filled with blankets, hats, greatcoats; little coats and even tables and chairs. Bed clothes, sheets and tents went whirling like leaves in the gale towards Sevastopol." When the storm abated and the morning of the 15th dawned, the full realisation of the damage became apparent: its destruction of the British base was absolute, far greater than the damage the Russians could impart. Not only was each regiment's camp wrecked, their tents and belongings strewn all over the peninsula, but also twenty-one British ships and fourteen French ships—agonisingly, with winter supplies for the army—were lost in Balaclava harbour.

It would get worse for the Allies: the winter that followed was one of the cruellest known in the Crimea. As they dug in to lay siege to Sevastopol, the harsh climate took its further toll on the men. Without adequate clothing and supplies, thousands more soldiers were lost during the winter months of 1854/55. The cavalry, too, were destroyed by the weather: horses, unable to cope with the conditions that were compounded by a lack of fodder, were lost in their thousands.

Advance Trench (Henry Clifford) (Royal Green Jackets Museum)

And if all that wasn't bad enough, medical facilities in the Crimea were a disgrace. There was a general hospital at a disused school at Balaclava, but at times it was crammed to five times its normal capacity with sick and wounded soldiers. Their agonising moans echoed around the shabby infirmary as they lay uncared for in desultory order. Russell informed the British readers of the conditions endured by those who had the misfortune to be incapacitated in the makeshift marquees:

> *Words cannot describe the filth. The commonest accessories of a hospital are wanting. There is not the least attention paid to decency or cleanliness – the stench is appalling. The sick tend to the sick; the dying, to the dying.*

If Russell was subjective he was certainly not inventive: he told the truth, and such truth did not sit well with the authorities.

The army was in desperate need of medical help and it came in a most unlikely form. It was not just white British men from humble backgrounds who would become heroes during the campaign. A mulatto woman from Jamaica called Mary Seacole would become the unlikeliest hero (or heroine, to be more precise) of them all. She would also become the darling of the troops for her commitment and tenacity in giving aid to the needy.

Florence Nightingale became the mythical heroine of the war: the lady with the lamp who, with her team of nurses, sailed to the Crimea after hearing about the appalling medical facilities. It is perfectly true that Florence did go on her mercy mission, but the hospital she took over at Scutari proved little more than a death trap for those poor enough to be shipped there from the Crimean peninsula; embarkation was poorly supervised and even then, the sick had to endure an agonising three-week voyage.

Mary, meanwhile, paid her own way from the West Indies to the Crimea after being refused permission to go by the British authorities. Her vocational will was illustrated still further when she then spent a further £800 of her own money to build 'Auntie Seacole's Hospital' in Balaclava. Her hospital was also primitive and rat-infested (rats were everywhere - that was a given) but the accommodation, supplies, meals and general tender loving care she offered to the troops marked her down as one of the most popular figures amongst the men. Statistically, if you were a sick soldier, you stood a greater chance of surviving under Mary's care than that of Florence's.

Assistant Surgeon Douglas Reid wrote admiringly of Auntie Seacole:

> She did not spare herself if she could do any good for the suffering soldiers. Through snow and rain, in storm and tempest, day after day, she was at her self-chosen post with stove and kettle.

The only time Mary was not at her post was when she was disappearing into the smoke, looking for the (allied and enemy) injured and wounded. The best thing that could happen to a soldier laid low with cholera, dysentery or typhoid was to be cared for on the spot in Mary's 'British Hotel', rather than endure the one-way package deal across to Scutari. And this is exactly what appears to have happened to Private Jacob Reed during January 1855. (In the muster rolls for his regiment he is listed with the 2nd Battalion in December 1854 and again in February 1855 but for the intervening month the word 'hospital' is entered. As it was a six-week round trip to Florence's hospital, plus recuperation time, Jacob could only have been in Mary's care during his short illness.)

Auntie Seacole's daily routine was to get the men up and serve them coffee and tea by seven o'clock. She would then pluck and cook her chickens, stew rhubarb, make broth, pies, and the soldiers' favourite, her milkless rice pudding. Such basic care of the young men, amidst the terrors of war, was of tremendous comfort. One wrote movingly:

Had you been fortunate enough to have visited the British Hotel upon rice pudding days, I warrant you would have ridden back to your hut with kind thoughts of Mother Seacole's endeavours to give you a sense of home.

Although Mary Seacole would go on to be awarded the Crimean Medal after the war, the spin-doctors of the day preferred to champion the story of the English rose and her lamp. (Mary virtually bankrupted herself because of her Crimean odyssey. After the war, those soldiers who had survived the horrors of sickness and slaughter did not forget their caring saviour. They organised regular fund-raising events for her benefit.)

Throughout the winter period, the Riflemen guarded the most advanced trench. Conditions were unimaginable; the Russian winters were like a malevolent force, like a glove closing in around anyone unfortunate enough to be exposed to them. Many men simply froze to death in the arctic conditions, giving up to sleep and becoming part of the oblivion, only to be discovered by their colleagues on the next shift; marauding enemy, under the cover of darkness, bayoneted others. Not surprisingly, there were reports of suicides amongst the men. Private Harry Blishen described one experience of such a shift:

I have just returned form the trenches, tired and almost worn out by incessant fatigues, and shocked at the awful spectacles of mutilated human flesh – for there had been three or four fellows literally blown to atoms this day.

Back with his colleagues, what would Private Reed be thinking as he went to do his shift in such conditions? In civilian life, he had escaped the horrors of the workhouse and the omnipresence of death and disease; now he found himself in this hell on earth. Just as things would seem to be getting better, such as an improvement in the weather, some other occurrence would dent morale and threaten the men's sanity. On 22nd April the lads of the 2nd Battalion were laughing and joking amongst themselves in the trench, buoyed by the improvement to the weather and a new 'it'll-soon-be-all-over' optimism. After much light-hearted argument and finger pointing, one of the young bandsmen, Private Wright, was nominated to go back to the camp to fetch water for his colleagues in the trench. Amid semi-serious 'I-went-last-week' protestations, Wright left his position to make the trip back. Within seconds he was shot and killed by a Russian sniper in his rifle pit opposite the British trench. Such was the constant threat to the survival of the British soldier in 1855. All levity among the Rifles died instantly with him and in one of those classic military historical red-mist

Mary Seacole c1855 (National Library of Jamaica)

moments, Wright's colleagues lost it completely: Riflemen Bradshaw, Humpston and Macgregor tore out of their trench under murderous fire and charged at the rifle pit, driving the Russians away and inadvertently moving the allies a few yards nearer Sevastopol. For this action the three men would each receive a Victoria Cross.

When he was not performing trench or picket duty, the task of the soldier was to bury his dead colleagues. During the winter this was a physically excruciating task and during the summer of 1855 it would be a physiologically torturous one. The sun was hot and bodies would swell to an enormous size, with their faces and hands burning black; becoming unrecognisable even to their friends. The stench was almost unbearable and the condition of the dead would naturally keep the disease cycle in constant motion.

To be a serving soldier in the Crimean War was a terrifying experience. The Russian guns were one thing; disease was something else. Throughout the summer months the men had to work harder to avoid cholera and dysentery. Fine young men in perfect health were taken ill with it and would die in four or five hours. One young officer of the 77th Regiment arrived on the Tuesday, was taken ill on the Wednesday morning and was buried later that night.

Back in the front line, Jacob's Rifle Brigade were preparing to lead the attack on the Great Redan, one of two forts that were key to the defence complex of Sevastopol. At this time, it is probable that Jacob was rubbing shoulders with other Carlisle lads and swapping stories about his home city, as the 34th Cumberland Regiment had been moved forward in preparation for the attack.

Throughout the summer several attempts were made to raise the siege of Sevastopol with its powerful, unbreached V-shaped defence work, whose defenders stood four deep behind the parapet. The first attempt came on 18th June when the British were to assault the Redan while the French would attack the Malakoff (the other main fort). The British chose this day as it was the anniversary of the Battle of Waterloo; if successful, it was felt that the day would be one of celebration thereafter on both sides of the Channel. The storming party consisted of Jacob's covering party from the Rifle Brigade, a ladder party from the Sailors' Brigade and the 34th Cumberland Regiment. It was Reed's job to keep the defenders under fire while the main attack went in (during the Napoleonic Wars this task was ominously referred to as the 'Forlorn Hope'). But the significance of the day was not lost on the Russians either. The defenders were ready for their enemy and as soon as the signal was given for the Allies to leave their

Guarding the Advance Trench (Henry Clifford) (The Royal Green Jackets Museum)

trench, they were showered with grape and shell. The attack was doomed to failure and not a ladder was placed at the foot of the Redan before the assault was aborted.

Among the besieged population inside the city was a young Russian artillery officer called Leo Tolstoy. Between bombardments, he was beavering away with his *Sevastopol Sketches* and would go on to use his experiences of the war as inspiration for his epic *War and Peace* (1875). Outside the besieged city, meanwhile, was a young Rifleman from Carlisle who wasn't much interested in writing his memoirs or seeking fame and fortune; he was simply interested in staying alive by dodging shot and shell, as the crescendo of violence built to its climax.

Allied losses were tremendous in the June offensive: three quarters of the men in the 34th Regiment alone were lost. A truce had to be called the following day to bury all the dead. The Allies were forced to resort to bombarding the city until a further Anglo-French assault was launched on 8th September. Again the Riflemen led off as skirmishers to draw the enemy fire. Soon regiments blended into one as they stormed the Redan, spurred on by the sight of the French tricolour flying over the Malakof. The Russians inside Sevastopol knew the game was up at this point and the south side of the city was evacuated at six o'clock in the evening after intensive all-day activity.

After 349 days, Sevastopol had been taken and victory was now a formality. But like so many, it was a hollow victory: the empty town was a scorched shell. The Russians retreated to be bombarded by the allied fleet for a further six months before the Armistice was signed on 29th February 1856. Evidence of how involved Private Reed and the Rifle Brigade were during the storming of the Redan came when many of their men were found dead after the fighting abated. Among them was the figure of Harry Blishen, the young man who ran away from home to enlist, stirred by a combination of pre-war jingoism and his own eagerness to serve his country.

Those who took part in the Crimean War received their campaign medals either during the war itself, or in due course. But the awarding of these medals and their battle clasps was not without controversy. Henry Clifford commented:

> I am surprised that many who were not under fire at the 'Alma' have been awarded; this is a sad mistake, or rather rule, in our service. It takes so much away from the gratification it gives to those who have exposed themselves so much and have been in such great danger to see their names mentioned on equal terms of commendation with those who looked on, and, who, though no doubt would have done as well if called upon, were not under fire at all.

While some questioned the merits of those deserving of the medal, other expressed their concern at the design and those of the clasps that had the main battles embossed on them. Colonel Hodge described them as:

> A vulgar looking thing, with clasps like gin labels. How odd it is, we cannot do things like people of taste. There should be a simple medal, given to those who were under fire in the trenches and to no other. These medals, given to all the world are of no value. They are too common.

Controversy as to who was involved and who looked on must have been a passing grievance for Private Jacob Reed, as the relief at coming through the bloody battles and surviving the squalid conditions would have outweighed the thought of their non-combatant colleagues being rewarded.

Reed and his Rifle Brigade, job done, travelled back to England in June 1856. In a bitter-sweet ceremony, Jacob's 2nd Battalion had the honour of parading before Queen Victoria herself on 26th June in Hyde Park. Jacob stood in the ranks of immaculately green-clad Riflemen, as he had once done at the Duke of Wellington's funeral. During the four intervening years he had witnessed less pomp and circumstance and more blood and thunder, but here he was now standing before this tiny woman, his sovereign, whose Empire he and his colleagues were duty-bound to defend. Eight of his colleagues stepped forward from the ranks that day to have the queen pin the highest military award to their tunic. (Queen Victoria approved the design and inscription of the Victoria Cross in January 1856. It was the first medal for valour open to both ranks of the services. The medals themselves were made from the melted-down Russian guns captured at Sevastopol. The awards ceremony in Hyde Park was the first time the medals were issued.) Would Jacob have been envious, as his colleagues marched past him to meet the queen? Would he have liked to be walking in their boots? One thing's for sure: Harry Blishen and thousands of others who didn't return would have given anything to be standing in his.

But if his experiences in the Crimea were starting to weigh heavily on Jacob's mind, he had little time to dwell on them. No sooner were the British task force landed back on home soil than they were again called on to shape up and ship out to another campaign. Less than a year after the cessation of hostilities with Russia, the very reason for the British involvement in the war (protection of its far-east interests) would rear its head: 1857 would be the year of mutiny in the jewel of the British Empire's crown, India.

Britain's history in India began in the sixteenth century when the Mughal Emperors reigned over the enormous country of patchwork regional—and lucrative—states. Two and a half centuries later and Britain controlled most of the country through the East India Company, an organisation that had started as a trading company but had gradually transformed into government by continually annexing independent states within its three 'Presidencies' of Bombay, Madras and Bengal. Greed and opportunism were endemic amongst the East India Company's employees and the Europeans who joined the Company were well aware that India was the place to be to fulfil their get-rich-quick philosophy.

The East India Company had had its own separate armed forces in each of its three presidencies. These armies were completely independent of one another and were paid for entirely out of the Company's Indian revenues; together they were larger that the British (or Queen's) Army. The Company army consisted of native troops, or sepoys, commanded by British officers who had been trained at the Company's military academy in England. They all enjoyed greater privileges and an altogether easier way of life within the East India Company than the soldiers whose lives lay within, and under the authority of, the regular British Army. It is for this reason that the officers in the Queen's army looked down their noses at their Indian counterparts.

By the 1850s, the Company were looking to annex the ancient independent province of Awadh in Bengal: its fertile valleys and populous towns made it one of the most prosperous and successful regions of all India. Its capital was Lucknow, with around 650,000 inhabitants.

Raising taxes, annexing and plundering independent states and treating sepoys with disdain all contributed to feelings of distress, hardship and anger amongst the indigenous peoples. Yet the British fatally continued to believe, up to and including the early months of 1857, that the local people and the sepoys, who outnumbered British soldiers by five to one, could not or would not do anything to disturb the status quo.

❋ ❋ 6 ❋ ❋

Upon their return from the Crimea the Rifle Brigade was issued with a new weapon. The new Enfield rifle was introduced to facilitate an accurate shot and enabled its operator to develop a quick rate of fire. The rifle itself would not prove controversial but the bullet used by the weapon certainly would. The self-contained paper cartridge contained both ball and powder charge. It required only the end to be bitten off and the cartridge then rammed down the muzzle of the weapon. To aid this process the cartridge was heavily greased with animal fat. Jacob and his colleagues were settling back into barrack-room life after the traumas of the Russian peninsula; the only immediate challenge that faced them was the mastery of the new rifle—not a major problem to skilled marksmen like these.

The British Empire was at its zenith and where its army led, its counterparts throughout the Empire followed. The intention was throughout the 1850s to introduce the new weapon to its forces throughout the globe. It was simply a natural progression in technology; what could possibly go wrong?

The first Enfield rifles had arrived in India in the spring of 1856. By January of the following year, rumours were circulating amongst the seventy-four regiments of native infantry (86,000 men in all) in the Bengal Army that these weapons signalled the intention of the British to convert all sepoys to Christianity. The rumours were that the grease used on the cartridge was a mixture of cow (sacred to Hindus) and pig (abhorrent to Muslims) fat. Biting such a cartridge would break the caste of the Hindu sepoys and defile the Muslims. These rumours were compounded further by tittle-tattle about the British who were allegedly polluting Indian (Hindu) food by grinding cow bones into the flour. These rumours were untrue but what mattered was that they reinforced the belief among the army personnel and civilians alike that Christianity was about to be imposed.

On the morning of 29th March 1857, at his regiment's barracks at Winchester, Private Jacob Reed was going about his normal business: rising, eating, training, parading—nothing out of the ordinary. Extra shooting practice was the order of the day with the Riflemen still familiarising themselves with their new Enfield. At the same time, half a world away in India, it was late afternoon, and another private soldier was (perhaps unknowingly) lighting a fuse that, once it reached its explosive, would have catastrophic consequences for thousands of Indians and Europeans, and would see the British Empire start a slow descent from its acme.

Mungul Pande was a young sepoy in the 35th Native Infantry Regiment in Barrackpore, a small town in Bengal near Calcutta. He was one of 257,000 sepoys throughout India, who were commanded by a mere 34,000 Europeans. On the afternoon in question Mungul Pande shot and wounded his sergeant major on the parade ground. As a result his regiment was disbanded. This might have been considered an isolated incident in London, but it proved enough to fan the flames of revolt amongst the natives across Bengal.

In Meerut, near Delhi, some six weeks after the events at Barrackpore, eighty-five sepoys of one of the finest native regiments, the 3rd Light Cavalry, to their shock and bewilderment were publicly disbanded for refusing to accept the new issue of cartridges. The men were humiliated, manacled and jailed.

By April the penny was starting to drop amongst government officials, so much so that they tried to have the sepoys make up their own grease from beeswax or vegetable oils. Moreover, in an attempt to remove any lingering objections the sepoys had concerning the new cartridges, their firing drill was altered. Instead of tearing the top of the cartridge with their teeth, like their European counterparts, the native troops could now do so with their left hand. It was too little, too late: the momentum after Barrackpore was unstoppable. The stage was set for the great tragedy to unfold.

Sir Henry Lawrence was the newly appointed Chief Commander in the Awadhi capital, Lucknow, having arrived in March 1857. He lived in the Residency, a large three-storey building, with several public buildings clustered round it. This was the heart of British officialdom in Awadh and with less than a thousand European troops serving with 7,000 sepoys, it didn't take long for Lawrence to recognise his perilous position. He wrote to Lord Canning, the Governor General of India, on 2 May warning that:

> *...until we treat Natives, and especially Native soldiers, as having much the same feelings, the same ambition, the same perception of ability and imbecility as ourselves, we shall never be safe.*

Eight days after Lawrence's letter, during the late afternoon of Sunday 10th May, British officers and their families were getting ready for Evensong in Meerut. A single shot rang out. A crescendo of noise almost immediately broke out in the native infantry lines. The sepoys came running out with guns, shooting every European in sight. They stormed the prison and released their jailed colleagues before going on a murderous rampage:

India c1857

soldiers and civilians, women and children — if they were British, they were fair game.

The long horror had begun. Many now view the greased cartridges as an excuse, as they were actually used against the British on that fateful night that saw the rising of the Indian soldiers and the killing of every Briton in the camp. News of the rising spread like wildfire throughout the country, unlike its journey back to the mother country. The time delay in communication from the sub-continent to London was painfully slow in 1857. First reports of the incident in Barrackpore were sketchy and this was followed by inaccurate correspondence printed in *The Times*; the *Carlisle Examiner* picked up the same story:

> *The Indian Army report a relatively minor problem within the ranks of the indigenous soldiers. It would appear that there was some objection to using the new Enfield rifle that was issued to all empire forces earlier this year. The strange event seems to have been*

addressed and the area around Calcutta has been completely subdued.

These reports however were printed in the middle of May, after the uprising at Meerut on 10th May. The events at Meerut had pre-empted the intentions of a group of Indians led by Nana Sahib, the Maharaja from the ancient town of Bithur, who had also planned to create an uprising in 1857. Nana's group were not some bunch of sub-continental yobbos; they were highly educated and wealthy natives who had witnessed some of the maltreatment of the country and its people by the British. His band of followers included his close advisor Azimullah Khan, his childhood friend Manu Bai (the Rani of Jhansi) and Tantia Topi, a Hindu Maharajah and a civilian, but also a ruthless guerrilla leader who trained Nana his military skills. A British barrister, John Lang, visited Nana Sahib's court shortly before the uprising and described the golden-robed Nana Sahib as 'a portly, sallow, expressionless thirty-year-old of medium height with an aquiline nose and large eyes'. He wrote of Tantia Topi: "He was a man of about middle height — say five feet eight — rather slightly made, but very erect. His eyes were expressive and full of cunning." These two figures were to become the key protagonists throughout the conflict.

Native civilians were all too willing to join with the mutinous sepoys and Nana Sahib and the smouldering fire of revolt slowly gathered pace around north and central India. It was soon to spiral out of control and descend into a maelstrom of violence.

Lucknow was taken within weeks but the most infamous and possibly blackest story of the rebellion occurred at the garrison of Cawnpore, between Delhi and Calcutta. Under the command of Tantia Topi 3,000 mutineers mutilated 300 Europeans, many of them women and children, and threw their remains down a dry well. Tantia focused the minds of potentially unwilling sepoys by threatening to have them blown from the guns if they did not obey his order to carry out the butchery. This happened on 27th June, the very day the British newspapers were reporting the outbreak in Meerut, six weeks earlier. (The Cawnpore massacre was not detailed until 15th July.)

When the relieving British army under Brigadier-General Henry Havelock arrived in an empty Cawnpore two days later to discover the barbarism, the soldiers were consumed with a blazing desire for retribution. As they discovered the brutality they went on an orgy of revenge murders and rapes. Locals were rounded up, beaten and smeared with cow's blood; some were even sown into pigskins before being executed. Muslims had pork forced down their throats and Hindus were forced to eat beef. Havelock ordered the captured sepoys should be executed by being tied to the mouth of cannon and blown to pieces.

As the beautiful country rapidly degenerated into bloody killing fields, rebel corpses were left hanging from trees to deter anyone from joining the mutiny. Within weeks, an empire which had taken centuries to create was shattered; its cities, with their stunningly beautiful domes and minarets, were smashed and ransacked, and its people turned into retribution-seeking maniacs.

The rebellious sepoy armies soon had control of Delhi, Cawnpore and the Awadi capital, Lucknow, some sixty miles north-east of Cawnpore, which contained 2000 people — 700 soldiers, 550 women and children and almost 800 non-combatants.

In England, as disbelief at the reported barbarism swept the nation, regiments prepared to sail, although the first infantry regiments to reach the Bengal Presidency did not do so until October of 1857. The reason for this was that Lord Panmure, the Secretary of State for War, was arguing over how to transport the troops to India. He claimed that steamships had to visit several ports to restock their coal supply, while sailing ships were able to shorten their course by keeping further off shore. (How did we ever win all those wars?) Once this imbecility was reversed and troop steamships were released, reinforcements — almost 40,000 — started to pour into Bengal. Until then, the authorities in India had to make do with troops transported in from Burma, Mauritius and China. There was also a substantial number of native soldiers still loyal: the Ghurkas from Nepal and the fierce-fighting Sikhs from the Punjab. When the Queen's Army did arrive from England to quell the rebellion, the Indians called it the 'Devil's Wind'.

✳ ✳ 7 ✳ ✳

Private Jacob Reed arrived in India on 27th October as part of the Rifle Brigade. The 2nd and 3rd Battalions were immediately ordered to Cawnpore to join General Charles Windham's outnumbered force. Windham was trying to defend the key city, which had already witnessed its fair share of tragedy throughout the summer months, after it had once again been taken into rebel control. The major forces of the loyal army were at the same time trying to secure the safe passage of women and children from Lucknow, some forty miles away.

The 3rd Battalion arrived at Cawnpore in early November and spent two nervous weeks waiting for the rebel attack that finally came on 27th November. As for Private Reed, he and the 2nd Battalion under Major Fyers approached the beleaguered city only to find the whole garrison in full retreat. Despite marching forty-nine miles in twenty-six hours, Reed and his colleagues were in the thick of the action, engaging the enemy while Windham and his troops tried to regroup. Heavily outnumbered, the British were forced to withdraw and the rebels took Cawnpore the following day. (In his regimental history of the Rifle Brigade, Basil Harvey states, "The endurance of these men in the subsequent campaign passes modern comprehension.")

A week later the Riflemen had regrouped under Sir Colin Campbell, the larger-than-life Glaswegian Lieutenant-General, whose experience of foreign campaigns was virtually unparalleled. Campbell was popular with his men, as they knew he valued their lives as much as his own. He had joined the Cawnpore operation after having successfully extricated the Europeans from Lucknow (although the city itself remained in rebel hands, at this time). The erstwhile roving reporter of the day, William Howard Russell, was again dispatched by *The Times* to cover the campaign, and was now also present.

Tantia Topi's Gwalior Contingent (numbering some 13,000) occupied Cawnpore. On 6th December the familiar order of 'Rifles to the front!' was given, as the British prepared to re-take the city. The centre and left of the rebel position was protected by the city itself. Campbell therefore had the Rifles feint an attack on the left before smashing through the relatively weak positions of the right. The plan worked brilliantly and the British soon had Tantia's men on the run. Whereas the rebels had seized the city through sheer weight of numbers a week earlier, Campbell re-took the garrison with his cunning, know-how and the awareness of his various regiments' strengths. Once the city was back in British hands the true horrors of what had occurred there dawned on the newly arrived soldiers. One wrote:

> *I felt as if my heart was stone and my brain fire, and that the spot was enough to drive one mad. All these fiends will never be repaid one-tenth of what they deserve.*

Thereafter, all reinforcements passed through Cawnpore, almost as an initiation to fire them up. Spurred on by popular opinion at home, the Queen's army saw themselves as dispensers of divine justice, and were out to repay the cruelty of the sepoys in kind. Fact and fiction blurred as anecdotes of slaughtered little angels and violated memsahibs spread throughout the ranks; every sepoy was a black-faced blood-crazed savage, who needed to feel the British wrath.

Between December '57 and March '58, Private Reed was involved in forced marches, sweeping the countryside for rebels and providing escorts for women and children on the dangerous stretch of road between Cawnpore and Lucknow. Conditions were difficult: cold nights and long periods without food (as long as thirty-six hours according to one report). Then on 2 March, Jacob mustered as part of Sir Colin Campbell's force, preparing to raise the siege of Lucknow. Although the British were 10,000 strong, they were preparing to attack a city of over half a million people held by a rebel force of 150,000. Maps of the city had been pored over; spies from within the city had filed their reports; Sir Colin now was content to march his army towards the capital of Awadh.

The colourful siege-train was formed by a caravan of kilted Highlanders, turbaned Sikhs, infantry regiments of the line, and cavalry and oxen drawing artillery of eight- and ten-inch guns for the Royal Artillery and the Naval Brigade. First out on to the dusty plain from Cawnpore was the cautious, skilful Campbell, accompanied by the 3rd Battalion of Riflemen. Two hours later, with the caravan stretching several miles in front of him, Private Jacob Reed and the 2nd Battalion the Rifle Brigade followed on as the rearguard.

By four o'clock on the blisteringly hot afternoon, the British were in sight of the city and Campbell halted the train and raised his binoculars. What he saw through the shimmering heat haze was the exotically beautiful city, with its skyline of azure domes and golden spires; of turreted towers that stood elegantly above the red terraced roofs. It was a city full of mystique that had witnessed, and was about to witness again, some of the most brutal behaviour, completely incongruous with this fairy-tale appearance.

Campbell, loath to waste unnecessary casualties in street fighting, decided to set up camp and utilise his artillery to its full potential; but after days of bombardment, he realised that an assault would have to be made by his foot soldiers. On 9th March the decision was made to attack at two o'clock in the afternoon. A flanking attack on the Dilkusha Bagh (a large villa in the centre of an extensive park) would be followed by an assault on the Sikander Bagh (a thick walled, castle-like enclosure about a hundred yards square, and one of the public buildings that clustered round Sir Henry Lawrence's Residency headquarters). The storming party would be a potent mix of Campbell's trusted Highlanders and the 4th Punjab Infantry Regiment. Incredible bravery was needed as the men were ordered to use no powder, just swords and bayonets, as their own artillery bombarded the right flank and the thick walls of the Sikander Bagh. William Howard Russell described the sun as 'a great red-hot cannon-ball,' as the men set off on their daring mission. As soon as the guns made a small breach in the thick walls, Sir Colin ordered the charge. Scotsmen and Sikhs almost fought one another to be first to get to the breach. The reward for the winners of this race was certain death; the first men through from both regiments were killed instantly, but that did not deter their colleagues from pouring through. Fortunately for Jacob, on this occasion the Rifles had not been ordered to lead the attack. Had this been the case, it is quite probable that his career would have ended there and then. As it was, with the breach secured, Campbell's army clambered over their fallen colleagues and into one of the key areas of the combat zone.

Half an hour into the assault the fighting was already brutal. During the fighting a British officer from one of the Sikh regiments was killed. His loyal native subordinates took retribution on the rebels responsible: storming a house from where the shots had come, they killed most of the sepoys but dragged one of their number out into the sandy street opposite the house. They punctured his face with their bayonets before building a small pyre and roasted their enemy alive. Officers and men looked on as the wretched creature tried to run off whilst ablaze—a human torch—but the Sikhs apprehended him again, threw him back on the fire, and held him down with their bayonets until his furious screams ended to signal the termination of the horrific scene.

On 11th March, with the city far from re-captured, a durbar (a state reception given by or for Indian princes) was held in honour of the Maharajah Jung Bahadur and his newly arrived force of Gurkhas. To us, this seems something straight out of *Carry On Up the Khyber* (while all hell is breaking loose around them, a group of English eccentrics are having afternoon tea, quite oblivious to the mayhem). In fact, it was customary to

Interior of the Sikander Bagh courtyard, Lucknow, 1858
(Felice Beato - Victoria & Albert Museum/V&A Images)

afford such a ceremonial welcome to the Maharajah, and Campbell no doubt felt it was worth spending a few hours wining and dining if it meant his army would be re-enforced by the hardy Nepalese fighters.

Campbell's forces pushed on through the city and progressed their assault towards the Residency, the region's symbolic heart. The infantrymen were operating in the most hazardous of conditions, as not only were they faced with an enemy that heavily outnumbered them but they were also in danger of 'friendly fire' as their own artillery bombarded the enemy positions. During the vicious street fighting that ensued, two Riflemen won Victoria Crosses.

There was also mass plundering during this period. Russell was appalled by the indiscipline of the British soldiers upon their entry into Lucknow; after witnessing them ransacking one of the buildings, he wrote:

These men are wild with fury and lust for gold. The British soldier is intoxicated with his thirst for revenge against the mutinous rebels and their cowardly acts against children and the memsahibs.

(An attempt to prohibit such indiscriminate plunder had been issued on 6th September 1857 when Brigadier Archdale Wilson issued a 'General Order' to that effect. In reality, it was widely ignored by officers and men alike.)

By the time the Residency itself was secured, it was a wreck. Walls had been knocked down, roofs had been blown off, and some buildings had completely collapsed under the incessant bombardment. Through the labyrinth of courts and back lanes — similar to those he was brought up in, in far off Carlisle — Private Reed and the Riflemen fought in ones and twos, alongside Highlanders and Sikhs, as the city was cleansed of rebel forces. The Sikhs especially continued their merciless retribution without any hesitation: doors were kicked in, houses were raided and enemy soldiers were dragged out from their hiding place to be bayoneted and burned. Russell's vivid description of one house leaves little to our imagination:

The scene was horrible. Sepoys lay in rooms, slowly burning in their cotton clothing, with their skin cracking and their flesh roasting literally in its own fat.

Russell continued to report the barbarous actions of the British Army and his editor back home printed his news but appeared at odds with his reporter, as he called for the execution of every mutineer in India! This view appeared to be shared by every British soldier who made the collective decision not to bother with prisoners once rebel positions were retaken: a little handiwork with the bayonet and sword was more appropriate, followed, of course, by the customary looting and plunder. (Later when trials were held, mutineers were either hanged or lashed to the muzzle of cannon and blown to pieces.)

When the dust settled on such carnage, it was discovered that two-thirds of the British community in Lucknow, including Sir Henry Lawrence himself, were dead. With the key cities of Delhi, Cawnpore, and Lucknow all secure, the task of the British was now to round up the scattered rebels, who were now to adopt guerrilla tactics which in turn would prolong the campaign for a further twelve months.

For their part, the Rifle Brigade made their base at Lucknow and took part in long sweeps for rebels, sometimes in extreme weather conditions, and sometimes in the company of cavalry. Members of the Royal Artillery were also present, one of whom was also a young man from Carlisle (his name is unknown). In June 1858, he wrote a letter home to his mother that was passed to the *Carlisle Examiner*. Not giving much thought to his mother's feelings, evidence of his and his colleagues' morale, and their longing for home, are explicit:

> *I write to let you know, thanks to God, that I have survived as hard a campaign as ever any British soldier has undergone in India….*
>
> *…We have had four companies of Rifle Brigade to reinforce us but conditions are terrible. Weather awful hot - thermometer rises to 140? in our tents. We have now had nine months under canvas and I am afraid we will remain so throughout the monsoon season. I will write again soon and hope to hear from you with a newspaper from home, however old it is.*

Food and water were at a premium, and a number of Jacob's 2nd Battalion were admitted to hospital during this period suffering from heatstroke and dehydration. Private Reed fortunately avoided illness and remained with his battalion throughout, unlike his experience and brief hospitalisation in the Crimea. During the joint patrols with the cavalry, the skirmishing Riflemen amazed their mounted colleagues by keeping pace with the horsemen. One officer from the 7th Hussars commented, "We couldn't get rid of those little green fellows!"

Despite such courage and resilience, the patrols carried out by the Riflemen proved largely fruitless. It was a tame end to a hard-fought campaign that had lasted for twenty months. Private Reed had marched 1,745 miles and he and his 2nd Battalion had the distinction of being the only battalion which, from landing in October 1857 until the last day of the Mutiny in July 1859, had been active in the field, as opposed to a period of inactivity in quarters. (Sir Colin Campbell had mixed fortune in his chase for Nana Sahib throughout northern India. He captured many rebels as he harried them into the jungles along the Nepalese border. Nana himself however, along with his associate, Azimullah, evaded capture and were never seen or heard of again.)

Lord Canning, the Governor of India, called for restraint, recognising the wrongdoing on both sides. His critics accused him of being a weather vane of a man, shouting him down and dubbing him 'Clemency Canning'.

Some experts differ on the correct terminology when describing the Indian uprising that was effectively confined to the Bengal Presidency. Some term it a full-scale revolutionary war, others a war of independence. It is mainly referred to however as the Indian or Great Mutiny. When studying the conflict, it is difficult to separate rights from wrongs, heroes from villains, and so easy to identify chances missed and tales of what-might-have-been. Though it dragged on for almost two years, it was effectively fought during a six-month whirlwind of murder and siege, heroism and brutality. During this period fifty-four of the seventy-four regiments in the Bengal Army mutinied or partially mutinied. The Bombay Army by contrast experienced only partial mutinies in only three out of twenty-nine native infantry regiments; the Madras Army had no mutinies at all. Civilians and soldiers, women and children were butchered on both sides and the avenging British Army was among the most incensed and cruellest sent out from British shores. (And those such as I who are fascinated by studying our ancestors' lives, and are determined to give them parity with some of the more well-known characters in history, have to accept that they too probably participated in such brutalities and injustices.)

To the military historian the Indian Mutiny is full of thrilling events and deeds of great valour, heroism and endurance. At the time however, Queen Victoria and the British government recognized that the mutiny had been born out of British misrule and a general lack of respect and was without doubt one of the most shameful chapters in the history of the Empire. Had it not been for the loyalty shown by the fierce-fighting Sikhs and Gurkhas the uprising would have been prolonged and the outcome might well have been very different.

The Queen herself was quick to realize the need for swift action and reconciliation and proclaimed on 1st November 1858, as the embers of the mutiny still burned, that her government would do everything possible to improve the moral and material welfare of the Indian people. (To a degree, and to Her Majesty's frustration, her statement remained a mere declaration of intent and it took many years for it to be put into practice.) One partial victory for the rebels was the disbanding of the East India Company, although a Secretary of State and the British Parliament remained responsible for governing India.

While the great and the good of Victorian officialdom argued the toss about how to deal with post-mutiny India, Private Reed and his Rifle Brigade returned to England.

Jacob Reed arrived back in England in August 1859. He had had a belly-full of soldiering by now; after experiencing the hardships of the Crimea and the sheer brutality of the Mutiny, like so many veterans of those campaigns, he decided to leave the army. Private Reed laid out his kit for the last time on 30th March 1860. He then collected what belongings he had and made the long journey back to Carlisle. The army he was leaving was then (and probably still is now) born of paradox. A soldier fought hard and was successful in campaigns, whose strategic purpose held little personal interest for him. Once his service was complete the army — for which he would have died — paid him scant regard. Like most career soldiers, Jacob had few skills that could be adapted for civilian life; so what was he going back to?

Nationally, the economy had rallied since the dark days of the 'hungry forties'. The fat cats who ran the factories were raking it in but one sinister angle of this resurgence was the disproportionately large number of women and — of greater concern — children, who made up the labour force. As the labour force consisted of of less confrontational personnel therefore, employee relations and civil disorder were less of a concern than they were during the early decades of the Industrial Revolution. This lack of confrontation also allowed employers to rethink their paternalism and room was made for organisations that would support and in some cases provide for employees, such as unions and friendly societies.

In Carlisle, the cotton industry was still the main source of employment for the inhabitants of the city. In Reed's absence from the nineteenth-century rag trade, the numbers who made a living from textiles was 4,225 (a sixth of the whole population, with over half the workers female). Jacob decided to swell the numbers by another one; after all this was all he knew, so it seemed as good a place as any to start. He set himself up again, after an eighteen-year absence, as a handloom weaver.

The city he had left twenty years earlier had changed (for the better) considerably. Sanitation had improved immeasurably, due in no small part to the formation of a joint stock company in 1846 that worked to supply water from the Eden at Stoney Holme, adjacent to its junction with the River Petteril. Through this work, the first adequate, unpolluted water supply for domestic use (and to service a sewage system) was introduced to the city, although as late as 1850 the Superintendent Inspector, Robert Rawlinson, was still scathing in his Report to the General Board of Health on the City of

Carlisle:

> *The working classes of Carlisle live almost entirely in lanes, courts and alleys between principal and secondary streets. Many of these lanes are entered by a covered passage and some are closed at one end. They are in general only a few yards apart with the doors opposite each. There is only one privy to the whole lane and these are ruinous and filthy.*

He went on in his typical pull-no-punches style, but it would not be long before his criticism, combined with The Carlisle Sanitary Association, who were still busy with their system of biennial and triennial inspections that had so shamed the authorities two decades earlier, started to deliver the goods. (The inspections continued until they were superseded by city administration and the appointment of a medical officer in 1874.) One contemporary commentator, writing ten years after Rawlinson, could not contain his enthusiasm for the improvements to living conditions:

> *There are few towns in England that have made more rapid strides in social and material advancement than Carlisle. In a single decade the face of the town has been almost entirely changed. Streets of houses, of massive form, with all the conveniences that modern art can suggest, have sprung up as residences for the merchant and the manufacturer, and the tradesmen. Streets of houses too, have been erected for the workingman, in lieu of dingy alleys, creaking garrets, and fever stricken yards. The clerk, the merchant, and even the labourer, has had his dwelling improved and now enjoys the freshness of the fields and the recreation derived from the cultivation of his little plot of garden ground.*

The wards of Caldewgate, Shaddongate and Denton Holme all benefited from such regeneration and it was one of these closely interwoven houses that Jacob rented with the money saved from his army career. Number 22 Morton Street was plain and small, but it was clean and had good sanitation; it was convenient as far as his occupation was concerned (a few hundred yards from Peter Dixon's cotton mill), and most important of all, it was his own. Jacob's working week followed a regular and familiar pattern: daily collection of yarn from Dixon's, working from home and weekly delivery of his products to the Peter Street Warehouse.

Sadly for Jacob and his like, one thing that hadn't changed was the paltry wage on offer to the handloom weaver. An unskilled labourer in London was taking home 18s per week. A handloom weaver in Carlisle would do well to make 10s. He would be paid by the piece and any faults

Denton Mill c1863 (Tullie House Museum & Art Gallery)

in the cloth detected by the cloth passer at the warehouse resulted in fines, which were deducted from his wages.

During his daily trips to the factory, Jacob met a young dryer, Mary Ann Benson, who at twenty-two, was half his age. With no time or inclination for much billing and cooing and a long courtship, the two were married within a year of his return home. And at the ripe old age of forty-four, Jacob Reed started a family with his new wife, when their daughter, Isabella (my great x2 grandmother), was born later that year.

But if Jacob thought his happiness was complete and his future secured, sadly, he had another think coming. Although the cotton industry was still the main source of employment in Carlisle, by the 1860s it had already started to decline. Reed had entered a profession whose numbers were dwindling, and worse was shortly to follow, due to events on the world stage.

In America the political climate was changing and this, as now, would have far reaching effects. In the same month that Jacob and Mary Ann celebrated the birth of their daughter, Abraham Lincoln was being inaugurated as President of the United States, on a ticket that opposed the further expansion of slavery. The southern states, whose cultural mantra was that of the white plantation owner benefiting from the work of the black slave, split away to form the Confederate States of America (with Jefferson Davis as president). On Friday 29th March 1861 the *Carlisle Patriot* carried a tiny paragraph—originating from the ubiquitous William Howard Russell, who was sent by *The Times* to cover developments—reporting that Lincoln was making no warlike movement 'but the seceding states are making energetic preparations for war.' (Did the editor fully understand the significance of this little piece, tucked away as it was on the inside page between similar sized paragraphs on events in Italy and Poland, and how the developing story would affect Carlisle?)

To make its bid for independence credible, the Confederacy embarked on its 'cotton diplomacy': lobbying for foreign recognition and support, especially from the two leading European powers, Great Britain and France, both of whom still were dependent on Southern cotton for their textile industries. (England, for example, imported 75 per cent of its cotton from the South).

After the customary let's-hope-it-all-goes-away period, Britain told Davis that it was unable to support something (slavery) they themselves had abolished half a century earlier. The government formally declared neutrality in the war and for good measure, forbade the construction of Confederate warships in British shipyards (but not before British cloth manufacturers had stockpiled large quantities of cotton). How ironic that a century earlier imports of cotton from across the oceans was the basis of the boom in the textile industry; then, British mill owners depended for their profits on the opening up of African markets for cheap cotton goods through triangular trade between Britain, Africa, and America, in which the movement of slaves was fundamental to the system.

When the hostilities began a month after Lincoln's inauguration (on 26th April the *Patriot* reported the commencement of hostilities to its Carlisle readership), supplies of raw cotton from the plantations virtually stopped. The American Civil War was to cost the lives of 620,000 men. Many crops were destroyed or confiscated, and much livestock was slain. More than $4 billion worth of property was wiped out. Britain's worst fears were realized when consequential ripples across the Atlantic pond turned into a tidal wave and its cotton industry went into meltdown, as southern plantation owners could not provide the resource or the material to satisfy the needy British. After only eighteen months of war most Lancashire mills had been completely shut down, which in turn led to mass unemployment, poverty and starvation.

Many historians now hold the view that that the cotton famine was caused as much by the over-production in the 1850s as the shortage of raw cotton from America in the 1860s, pointing the finger at the owners who began mill closures and short-time working as they were unable to sell all the cloth they had made and stockpiled. Whether it was the boom or the bust; either way the bell tolled for the industry in Britain. Once victorious, the US Congress enacted much of the legislation to which the South had objected so strenuously before the war, including that of emancipation of the black slaves: nearly four million became 'free'.

In Carlisle, as in Lancashire and elsewhere, the cotton famine of the 1860s saw the businesses of local textile barons like the Dixons and the Fergusons dwindle—something that had taken generations of their families to build up was now frittering away to nothing in a couple of years. And if the Dixons and the Fergusons of this world were to be affected, then the Reeds were also. Jacob was in fact one of the lucky ones, due to the little money he had earned from his army career, and his established home on Morton Street. He managed to struggle through, continuing to weave until the last possible moment. That moment came seven years after the end of the American Civil War, the death-knell of the British cotton industry. Dixon's business was reliant on the cottage industry that saw Jacob and the like working from home. As handloom weavers were increasingly being superseded by the factory system, Dixon was declared bankrupt in 1872. (As for Ferguson, the male line died out and was taken over by the Chance family, into which one of the Ferguson daughters had married. Frederick Chance was not put off by the problems of the '60s, as he pioneered new systems of dyeing and finishing, as well as building a spinning mill and weaving shed at their Holme Head factory. His courage and foresight enabled Ferguson to become a fully integrated cotton manufacturer that ran successfully well into the twentieth century.)

One thing the cotton famine did not do was to put off Jacob making up for lost time in the family stakes. Regular little Reeds appeared throughout the 1860s: John, William, Robert and Jane all arrived before the end of the decade, and he wasn't finished there; Jacob and Mary Ann's youngest daughter, Katherine, was born in 1872. One advantage the children had over their parents was a form of schooling, as they benefited from significant government change to the education system. School boards were introduced in 1870 as part of the Education Act, while grants to church schools were doubled. By the middle of the decade almost 5,000 children throughout the city were being educated in schools that even catered for different denominations. The Reed children attended Trinity School in Caldewgate.

Now fifty-five years old, Jacob Reed reverted to labouring to earn a living. His wife Mary Ann, however, continued to work in the dwindling textile industry as 'women's work' (dyeing and bleaching, spinning and woollen machining) prevailed.

Fortunately for the city's economy and workforce, the decline in the cotton industry occurred simultaneously with the second coming of the railways. The first had taken place in the 1840s with the Lancaster to Carlisle line being the highlight. (This period saw the diminishing usefulness of the Carlisle Canal that had hitherto acted as the city's main goods transportation source, but was reliant on tides and restricted harbour facilities to accommodate the growing needs of the expanding Border City. Ironically, the canal itself was eventually filled in and replaced with a railway.)

Now, two decades later, the Midland Company was seeking to compete with their great rivals, London and North Western, and in September 1866, work began on the Settle to Carlisle Railway. In his hilariously funny travel book, *Notes From a Small Island*, Bill Bryson describes the Settle to Carlisle Railway as a 'folly; it runs from nowhere much to nowhere much by way of nothing at all.' This may be true, for as Bryson points out, there was already an east coast line and a west coast line, so why drive another one straight up the middle? But James Allport, General Manager of the Midland Railway decided to do just that, and Carlisle would be eternally grateful for his folly.

Within the next ten years Carlisle would establish itself as a major rail hub. With a steady increase in goods trains and well over a hundred passenger trains frequenting its Citadel Station (1848) every day, the station was enlarged in 1873 and goods traffic was diverted west of the station through the Denton Holme and Caldewgate suburbs. This freed up the station to safely accommodate more passenger trains and within a further three years, express trains running north from London to Glasgow and Edinburgh were stopping in the city. With this level of growth, it is no surprise that the railways became of prime importance in ensuring the city's industrial future. The *Carlisle Guide* of 1881 emphasised the point when referring to the progress in manufacturing, and the subsequent upturn in the economy:

> *Railways gave the impetus to these strides of prosperity, which have gone on contemporaneously with the prosperity of the system that called them into existence. Carlisle is now a great centre of railway communication. East, West, North, South the iron roads radiate from it. It is placed on two of the three great trunk lines which run from one end of the kingdom to the other, and has short and easy access to the eastern and western seas.*

Caldewgate and Holy Trinity Church, Carlisle, late 19th century (Carlisle Library)

Caldewgate in the late 19th century, from the tower of Holy Trinity Church. (Carlisle Library)

To facilitate such major change, of course, a further influx of labour was required and the 1860s and 1870s saw more Scottish and Irish immigrants come into the city; a city whose population would be bumped up to over 35,000 by the end of the decade. One such individual was William Thompson, an engine fitter from Scotland. He came to the city as part of the Caledonian Railway Company's expansion of its operation in Carlisle. In the same year as the enlargement of the station, the Caledonian spent a further £20,000 in building its new engine sheds and wagon repairing shop on Kingmoor Road.

It was William who would catch the eye of Isabella, Jacob's eldest daughter, and the two were married in 1880. The first of Jacob's four grandchildren—also Mary Ann—was born the following year.

POSTSCRIPT

One thought that continually troubles me when looking through my family history is: should I be doing this at all? None of us like people poking their noses into our affairs, and we are in a position to protect our interests; those in the past have no comeback. It is with this thought in mind, therefore, that I feel that old Jacob appears to have had the last laugh on his inquisitive great (x3) grandson. This is because we don't actually know when or where he fell on life's great battlefield. The usual avenues of exploration open to the genealogist (St Catherine's House Index, International Genealogists Index, church records, burial records etc) refuse to throw up any clues regarding his passing. All we have to go on is the 1891 census that lists Mary Ann as a widow. The probability is that Jacob died sometime during the mid 1880s and was buried in the local churchyard, although Trinity Churchyard was full to capacity by this time.

If this is a mystery, what is not is the certainty that his dependants continued their austere, unforgiving existence. After Jacob's death, his widow, Mary Ann, and her youngest daughter, Kate, moved in with Isabella and son-in-law William Thompson. By 1888, William and Isabella had their own family: two boys and two girls. Tragedy struck the family again when, in the same year, William was killed in a railway accident. Thus, 28-year-old Isabella Thompson was left to support a mother, a sister and four children on the meagre wage of a power loom weaver. Any financial security that Jacob accrued during his life soon evaporated as his widow and daughter fought to survive. Mary Ann died on 23rd April 1898 aged sixty—she was buried in a pauper's grave.

The world scene had changed dramatically during Jacob's lifetime. Both the Russian and Ottoman empires were practically bankrupt through the Crimean War, and although Reed lived to see the British Empire rise to its zenith, he was spared its dramatic fall; not that he and his like ever benefited from being subjects of the largest empire the world had ever known. The story of the Reeds, the Thompsons, and many like them is cyclical and familiar: cotton and Caldewgate, hardship and injustice, tragedy and anonymity. I'm left believing that those who pontificate about 'the good old days' had the good fortune of never having actually experienced them.

ISAAC SCOTT

Tailor & Private with the 17th Lancers

❋ ❋ 1 ❋ ❋

Of course, one of the main avenues for any genealogist to explore is that of the biographical anecdotes of bygone family members, passed down by subsequent generations. Equally, one of the occupational hazards for family historians is when the avenue of exploration becomes a blind alley or even worse, a dead end, when you discover that the anecdote is incorrect. Such was the case with Isaac Scott, who was the original inspiration for this particular historian's interest in his own ancestry. Family legend had it that Isaac took part in the Charge of the Light Brigade, the famous action that was part of the Battle of Balaclava during the Crimean War of the mid 1850s.

The initial discovery that Scott was not actually one of the famous six hundred naturally came as a surprise and (I must confess) a huge disappointment, but further investigation revealed that the young man from Penrith was well worth his place in the history books — at least, the family history books — as his full time and part time military career would last for over twenty years and see him following the trail of Jacob Reed, serving in Eastern and Western Europe, as well as spending ten years in India.

Isaac was actually born in Cockermouth on 22nd June 1834, the first son of William Scott who had married Agness Key the previous year, at All Saints' Church in the town. Their second son, Joseph, was born two years later.

The Scott family had farmed in the Cockermouth area for generations. William himself was born as another more famous son of the town was wandering lonely as a cloud in the early years of the nineteenth century. The fifty-year period prior to William's birth had seen the agricultural industry witness the Agrarian Revolution. Gone was the traditional three-field system of farming that dated back to the Middle Ages which saw the fields divided into several strips with farmers cultivating strips from a number of plots. Although this system shared out the land equally, it was an inefficient way of farming as the farmers themselves had no enclosed land and had to constantly travel back and forth between their strips in different fields. In the latter half of the eighteenth century, the enclosures lobby achieved greater success in progressing Enclosure Acts through Parliament: by joining the strips in the open fields to make larger compact units of land, the farmer was now allowed to work in one area. With this greater independence, an increased choice of what to grow and its production in larger volumes, the individual began to see his profits increase.

This major change in the industry, along with the advent of machinery (prior to 1750, all farming was done by hand) not only benefited the individual farmer, but the country also. A country embroiled in the Napoleonic Wars demanded more crops; a farmer whose limits of cultivation had been extended (it is estimated that 12 million acres were under arable cultivation in 1812) could grow more food to feed its domestic population. The only downside for the farmer was that his landlord was allowed to charge the tenant a higher rate for the enclosed land.

The boom being experienced in the cotton industry at this time was thus mirrored in agriculture, making Cumberland an attractive destination for all those early-century immigrants. And if the urban classes relied on the textile industry for employment, then their rural counterparts relied on agriculture for theirs. It was the biggest single source of employment in the mid nineteenth century, providing work for over a fifth of the working population of Britain.

The county in particular, throughout the early years, witnessed its agriculture industry thrive. The 1829 *Cumberland Directory* enthused:

> The agriculture in Cumberland as well as Westmorland has, within the last thirty years, been brought to a high state of perfection, and now considerable quantities of corn are exported. Long memories are required to recollect the days of great amounts of importation taking place.

When William Scott married in 1833 he was one of 300 tenant farmers in and around Cockermouth. His wife was Agness Key; the Key family being a long established family in nearby Lorton (her grandfather , the wonderfully named Mirehouse Key, was one of the more influential characters in the area for the final forty years of the eighteenth century).

But further change was afoot in the Cockermouth area, as over the next four years, the Earl of Lonsdale, taking advantage of the 1832 Reform Bill, set about purchasing the burghers' tenements from their respective owners and appointing his friends as the new 'owners'. As middle class landowners had greater voting rights under the Reform Bill, the Earl was virtually guaranteeing himself continuous parliamentary election victories by such cronyism.

William therefore found himself looking elsewhere to ply his trade. He found it thirty miles to the east of his home town. The east of the county was by the 1830s seeing an expansion in its arable land, with the large area between Penrith and Carlisle, until then, part of the Inglewood Forest, being bought and prepared for husbandry. The market town of Penrith itself had seen its population double to just fewer than 6,500 from the turn of the century to the time of Victoria's accession in 1837. The Penrith Agricultural Society was formed in 1834 for the purpose of improving breeds of livestock, and the Penrith farmers were a tightly knit community. The highlight of their year was their annual show held in August, described by one commentator as one of the best exhibitions in the North of England. In 1838 William Scott took the courageous decision to join them by moving his young family from Cockermouth to take up the lease on the larger property of Fernside Farm, just outside the town.

The one key factor that defined agriculture during the first half of the nineteenth century was the Corn Laws: a series of statutes enacted between 1815 and 1846 which kept corn prices at a high level. This measure was intended to protect English farmers from cheap foreign imports of grain following the end of the Napoleonic Wars. ('Corn' meant grain of all kinds, not simply vegetable corn.) When the law was introduced, it stated that no foreign corn would be allowed into Britain until domestic corn reached a price of 80 shillings per quarter. Farming therefore became extremely lucrative, and farmland was traded at very profitable rates.

The Corn Laws were never intended to be an unmitigated benefit for the producer, nor an unmitigated penalty for the (either rural or urban) consumer. They were simply designed to set the threshold price above which corn could be imported. The reality was that the main beneficiaries of the Corn Laws were, of course, the nobility and other large landholders who owned the majority of profitable farmland. The people living in Britain's fast-growing towns, who had to pay higher prices for bread, hated the legislation. The industrial classes saw the Corn Laws as an example of how Parliament passed laws that favoured large landowners. If you were a 'have' (a landowner), you had a vested interest in seeing the Corn Laws remain in force; if you were a 'have not', you had to spend the bulk of your income on corn just to survive.

Since the lower classes had no income left over for other purchases, they could not afford manufactured goods. As a result, manufacturers suffered and had to lay off workers; these workers had difficulty finding employment, so the economic spiral worsened for everyone involved. Finally, as we have seen, the right to vote was not universal, but rather depended on land ownership, and, rather like turkeys' reluctance to vote for Christmas, the land-owning Members of Parliament had no interest in repealing the Corn Laws. In short, the Corn Laws were a very contentious issue, and one of the main issues to be addressed at the meeting organised at St Peter's Field, Manchester, on 16th August, 1819 — the event that became known as the Peterloo Massacre. The job of the William Scotts of this world was therefore to tug the forelock and make the best of what they had; and possessing shrewd business acumen, William did this with some success, despite remaining a tenant farmer.

It was commonplace for farms to be passed from father to son during the eighteenth and nineteenth centuries; providing the land was cultivated reasonably well, they behaved in a responsible manner and they paid the rent on time to their lords and masters on a regular basis, families could go on leasing farms for generations. In many cases this was mutually beneficial to both parties, as it rarely paid farmers to put their resources into buying the land when money could be used for extending the scale of their operation. Most were content to be tenants, seeing their capital produce a good return whilst feeling secure under a good (if sickeningly wealthy) landlord. William employed three farm labourers to help with the bigger site and the keeping of livestock.

In the run-up to the 1840 General Election, the Whig government, under constant pressure from Chartists, the Anti-Poor Law movement and the Anti-Corn Law League, set up a Parliamentary Select Committee to investigate the actions of import duties. Sir Robert Peel (Leader of the opposition) asked scathingly on the eve of the election:

> *Can there be a more lamentable picture than that of a Chancellor of the Exchequer seated on an empty chest, by the pool of bottomless deficiency, fishing for a budget?*

The Conservatives won the election and Peel became Prime Minister but was not so smug when faced with managing the thorny problem himself. The Anti-Corn Law League — the prototype pressure group whose members were mainly middle-class manufacturers, merchants, bankers and traders — continued to pressure the government to repeal the Corn Laws so that they could sell more goods both in Britain and overseas. The repeal movement was increasingly convincing Peel, who believed that British farmers could compete with foreign imports.

As the seemingly endless debates about the Corn Laws continued, the Penrith farmers established their own club in 1845 for 'the discussion of agricultural topics and the advancement of interest of farmers and agriculturalists generally'. The following year the farmers found they had something meaningful to discuss: after decades of unrest, and in the immediate aftermath of the catastrophic potato crop failure in Ireland, Peel repealed the Corn Laws. (The controversy over this measure was so great, however, that Peel was forced to resign).

This was a seminal moment, not only for the country but also for William Scott. He had shown himself to be a shrewd businessman in his decision to move from Cockermouth, as there was a greater potential in this area of the county: not only was Penrith a larger town, but also rural east Cumberland had many mines, and oats and hay produced on the farms provided fodder for the colliery horses, whilst some of the grain and livestock was sold directly to the pitmen. His first eight years in the Penrith area had proved successful, but now he faced the dilemma of what to do in the face of such a radical change (and potential threat) to his profession. Despite their repeal, the Corn Laws continued to polarise the country.

Scott belonged to the deeply suspicious body that believed that the abolition of the Corn Laws and the arrival of cheaper grain, flour and bread would be a pretext for employers to lower wages. If this happened, the inevitable consequences would be a post-repeal depression in the farming industry. So, after much deliberation, William took the characteristically brave decision of giving up what had been his and his family's occupation for generations and move into the town itself, buying the Grate Inn, from the estate of Mary Stubbs, one of no less than fifty-four public houses in Penrith around the middle of the nineteenth century. (The 'great depression' in agriculture so feared by Scott would not actually materialise for another thirty years.)

The Grate itself was situated on Netherend (later Front Street, now King Street). The Scotts' new property, like most hostelries of the day, had stables to the rear. The farmers — no doubt including William himself — would come into the town on market days and park their horse and carts or traps at the rear of their favourite tavern, do their business in the market place and retire to their place of relaxation, where it was not unknown for further trading to take place amongst the clientele.

As well as the stables, the new landlord inherited Thomas Brustead, a 37-year-old lodger who worked as a saddler in the stables, and Annie Little, a live-in servant. Domestic service was heavily relied upon during the Victorian period. Certainly every middle-class family had their own 'Upstairs Downstairs', as nationally the numbers of domestic servants exceeded the numbers of textile workers in every census. In the mid-Victorian years between 1851 and 1871, the number of domestic servants increased by 60 per cent, twice the rate of increase of the population).

The Grate Inn (John Thompson) (Penrith Library)

The Grate had two other interesting features: one was an exterior flight of steps that led to the living accommodation on the upper storey; the other was a barber's shop, run by Thomas Stewart, that fronted the building. Both William and Thomas found their names printed in Mannix and Whellen's *The Principal Inhabitants of Cumberland* in 1847. The two were to remain friends and working neighbours for over twenty years as both men enjoyed success in their respective businesses.

Scott's two sons, Isaac and Joseph, were educated at the National School for Boys founded in 1833. They were part of the first generation of working-class people who benefited from any kind of decent schooling after the first financial grants for education were made available to the Church by the government in 1832, the watershed year of reform. The Scott brothers' more intelligent (or perhaps more fortunate) contemporaries received their education at the Free Grammar School of Queen Elizabeth, founded in the mid sixteenth century. The curriculum at such schools was based on the classical Latin and Greek studies from the Elizabethan era, but the teaching received by the two boys simply consisted of reading, writing, religious instruction and basic arithmetic.

The education for all classes of youngster boded well for the future of a town that continued to develop into the mid-Victorian period; that was until that old nineteenth-century pest, cholera, came calling. Whereas Penrith was not in the same league as Carlisle for nineteenth- century filth and squalor, the small market town was not completely exempt from death, disease and decay. The disease ravaged the town during 1848 and this prompted the residents to hold a public meeting on the question of public health and hygiene. William attended this meeting on 18th October 1848 where a board of health was appointed to 'superintend and direct the cleansing of the town' under the Public Health Act. This board soon found that it had no powers to raise funds for the extension of drains; and the killer disease continued to have its way with the residents for a further twelve months.

Despite the obvious health problems, the Penrith business community opposed the implementation of the Act, claiming it would 'inflict the expensive machinery of the Act on property already burdened with a heavy load of taxation.' As the inhabitants voiced their opposition to the act, Robert Rawlinson, Superintendent Inspector, became the focal point of attention as he instituted an enquiry into the state of Penrith's sanitation.

His report was not published until 1851 but the locals had to accept the inevitable, for he strongly favoured the adoption of the Act in the town. His report left no one in any doubt as to what was required:

> *A complete system of sewers and drains; a full water supply, constant and at high pressure; a pipe and tap, complete, taken from each house and room tenement, the removal of all solid refuse at short intervals; to provide means for applying the sewer refuse on the land, for agricultural purposes; better pavement in the public streets, and pavement or flagging in all passages, courts and yards, with regular cleansing at short intervals;*

The report concluded:

> *The sanitary condition of the parish of Penrith is very defective; that to insure health to the highest degree, the houses require to be drained, and the stream through the town to be freed from pollution.*

The report was strenuously opposed by many of the townsmen but their protests were to no avail and the Act was applied on 25th June 1851.

✳ ✳ 2 ✳ ✳

The first indication of young Isaac Scott's long-term military ambitions came in the same year that Rawlinson's searchlight was piercing the fog of Penrith's sanitation problems. Having completed his basic schooling shortly after his fourteenth birthday, and while his elders and betters were in deep discussion about the town's health and well being, he left his parents' home without their knowledge and ran away to the Royal Barracks in London, where he attempted to join the army by lying about his age. Little did he know that his mother was in hot pursuit. Upon finding the note from her son explaining his disappearance, Agness made the 14-hour train journey to the capital, whereupon she went straight to the barracks and explained the situation to the recruiting officers, who had the young boy brought out and returned to his mother. She, no doubt after pointing out to him the error of his ways, returned with her son home to Penrith. As suggested earlier, the 1840s was a period of intense recruitment into the army due in no small part to the abject poverty that existed amongst the lower classes. Scott, however, did not fall into such a category, being from a relatively wealthy family and having a basic education. His actions therefore tend to support the theory that, unlike Jacob Reed, Isaac was genuinely interested in pursuing a career in the military from a very young age.

In an attempt to help their son settle down, Mr. & Mrs. Scott approached Mr. William Turner who plied his trade as a tailor in his own shop on Angel Lane in the town. Turner was agreeable to their request for an apprenticeship for their eldest boy, and as a result Isaac started working for him in September 1849.

During the following five years, while Isaac developed his skills with cloth and thread, the army he so desired to be part of was moving towards its first major campaign in 40 years. When the Crimean War did break out, the young apprentice had to be satisfied with sitting in his employer's shop reading about it. By November 1854 the reports sent back from the Crimea by William Howard Russell of *The Times* were filtering into the provincial newspapers, amongst which were the *Carlisle Journal* and the *Penrith Herald*. An example of one report in the *Journal* was printed on 3rd November 1854, informing the reader of the commencement of the siege of Sevastopol. In the same piece Russell emphasised the desperation for extra resource, noting the cavalry were seeking to procure horses of four years old rather than the traditional three, thus allowing them to be trained more quickly.

Furthermore the bounty for each soldier had been raised and the height requirement for each serviceman had been reduced by an inch. It may have been these reports through which the young apprentice tailor fuelled his desire to pursue a career in the military.

Or could his inspiration have come from a source rather closer to home? Across the road from the Grate was the Mitre Hotel, once owned by a local man called Pearson, whose own son, William, had joined the 4th Light Dragoons in 1848. Trooper Pearson was with his regiment in the Crimea and they were part of the famous Light Brigade that charged at Balaclava. Pearson wrote home to his parents and his letter was printed in the local paper on 18th November 1854 (three weeks after the charge) detailing his experiences on that fateful day. No doubt Isaac read about his former neighbour who commented on the:

> ...shells, bullets, cannon balls, and swords that kept flying around us. The Russians fight well but we will make them yield yet.

No doubt either, that Isaac's mother, still vehemently opposed to her son's ambitions, read the piece and focused on Pearson's darker comments:

> Dear mother, every time I think of my poor comrades, makes my blood run cold, to think how we had to gallop over the poor wounded fellows lying on the field of battle, with anxious looks for assistance — what a sickening sight!

Isaac was now twenty years old and could wait no longer. It was March 1855, and although it was four months before the completion of his apprenticeship, Scott informed both his employer and his parents, with whom he was still living at the time, that he intended to leave home and volunteer for service in the Crimea. Agness was distraught by her son's decision; whether or not it was simply a mother's intuition, she had a strange sense of foreboding. She had just cause: her eldest son said his goodbyes in April 1855 and she was destined never to see him again.

On 10th April 1855 the 5ft 6 fi inch, 20-year-old apprentice tailor from Penrith became Private 1622 Isaac Scott of the 17th Lancers; one of the most glamorous and famous regiments in the British Army. Although his was obviously a different regiment from that of his townsman, Pearson, both the 4th Light Dragoons and the 17th Lancers were Light Cavalry and therefore part of the Light Brigade that charged at Balaclava. (This tends to support the theory that it was Pearson's mounted exploits that inspired Scott).

The 17th Lancers had been in existence for almost one hundred years by the time of the Crimean War. Their regimental motto was a Death's Head emblazoned with the words 'or Glory', which gave the members of the regiment their nickname: the 'Death or Glory Boys'.

The cavalry's aim in eighteenth and nineteenth-century warfare was to ride down fugitives, capture or kill them and ensure that a broken enemy remained broken. The Light Cavalry evolved to push the pursuit yet faster and further, often following up engagements taken on by Heavy Cavalry or Infantry. Light Cavalry were also equipped to act more effectively than Heavies in the role of scouts and in small skirmishes. Although the cavalry regiments saw themselves as the elite of any army, the truth was that they could not function effectively without working directly with, and in some cases being totally dependent on, the infantry. Not that this would ever be conceded by cavalry officers who were either boorish snobs or hoity-toity buffoons with mutton-chop whiskers, who spent virtually all the their time trying to outdo each other.

Light Cavalry regiments consisted of men of 5ft 6ins to 5ft 8ins in height and English thoroughbred horses bred for speed, manœuvrability, and the ability to carry up to 200lbs in weight. Its men were the smartest in the British Army; their exotic uniforms were developed from the eastern cavalry, with the 17th wearing blue tunics faced and piped in white with a cross belt and grey overalls. Their distinctive square topped chapka (helmet) was adopted from the Polish Army. The lance they carried weighed just less than four pounds and was a standard length of nine feet.

Isaac enlisted into the regiment at Brighton where their home headquarters were at that time, signing up for twelve years' regular service. He was a welcome addition as the regiment was desperately in need of recruits at the time, having been reduced to less than three dozen fit and able men in the field.

Although they were unknown to one another, Scott was to follow the routes trodden by Jacob Reed, but their experiences, both on the battlefield and in the barrack room, were to be very different. If the living conditions for Jacob Reed and his infantrymen colleagues were appalling, the barrack room of Isaac Scott and his cavalrymen colleagues was worse. Their billets were situated above the stables, so upon entering you not only experienced the foul odours of what the human body has to offer, but also the rising aroma contributed from their equine counterparts down below.

Despite the eagerness of such new recruits and their desire to join the regiment in Russia, and despite the regiment crying out for extra personnel, they naturally had to go through a certain amount of training before being allowed to take up arms.

If you were a new recruit, your working day was a long one. It began with waking to the sound of the trumpet (as opposed to the bugle that was used in the field of battle) that sounded morning stables at a quarter to five. There followed half an hour for washing, dressing and making good your bed before going downstairs to shake out the litter and generally prepare the horses for the day's activities. Having changed into riding gear, it was then time for mounted training, which was the terror of most recruits, many of whom had never sat on a horse before enlistment.

Isaac was one of the exceptions to this rule. Having been raised on a farm his natural horse skills made him a perfect recruit for the under-resourced cavalry, whose main body was still being decimated half a world away. Country boys such as he were easier to train, as during the first few weeks no saddle was allowed, and it would be several more before the men used stirrups. They were not expected to spend endless hours learning high school riding techniques but actively encouraged to ride the way they knew: with the horse's head pushed forward, allowing a long easy stride. Their less-experienced colleagues from urban backgrounds suffered for months at the hands of heartless instructors, who openly stated that their aim was to give their pupils as many falls as possible in order to prepare them for their career ahead. More stables followed at eleven o'clock till lunch. Afternoon was given over to foot drill, arms drill and gymnastics. The regiment had to be ultra smart in every detail of dress and equipment, and once tea was taken at five, and following third stables, the troopers would spend time cleaning their uniforms before retreat (bed-time to you and me) was sounded at ten.

As the recruits became more proficient on horseback they progressed to the open areas where they had to perform every type of mounted manœuvre whilst maintaining formation with their colleagues at varying pace. The variations on manœuvres ran into dozens. Often at the end of a morning's session the regiment would form up for a mock charge, which was every cavalryman's dream to perform in battle.

At close quarters there were 20 sabre positions to be executed: Light Cavalry troops carried a curved sword about 36 inches in length and 1/ inch in width. They differed from their Heavy colleagues who carried a straight sword with the same dimensions. Each of these moves had to be learned and practised to perfection, as did the handling and use of the lance. The lance was originally made of ash but as this tended to warp, especially in hot climates, male bamboo was adopted in 1836. The pennons were small flags fastened just below the steel tip of the weapon and denoted the national colours, red and white being those of the British Army. It was not only a controversial piece of equipment but it was also an awkward weapon to master, with the recruits not only having to learn to ride whilst carrying the weapon but also learning seven primary movements that might have to be adopted in battle. Critics claimed that it was an impractical implement of war, given that it was useless without being backed by a charge. In the stationary position the carrier had no penetrative power and he had no alternative but to resort to the use of his sword. Other regiments scornfully referred to the weapon as a 'spear'. Nevertheless in the hands of a well-trained trooper the lance was an especially effective weapon, ruthlessly so when pursuing a fleeing enemy, as Scott himself was to witness and demonstrate later in his career.

✳ ✳ 3 ✳ ✳

As Private Scott was going through his basic training, the forces in the Crimea were in desperate need of reinforcement as the war was taking a heavy toll. William Howard Russell was at odds with the home authorities; in his *Times* reports he would constantly contradict the rhetoric put forward by the establishment concerning the British forces. 'On the eve of the battle of Balaclava,' he wrote, 'the army of 35,600 had been reduced to no more than 16,500, with forty to fifty men being lost to cholera each day.'

The finest light horsemen in Europe had been reduced to a shattered group of soldiers. The 17th totalled only 35 troopers after the battle of Balaclava, a battle that included the famous Thin Red Line, the Charge of the Heavy Brigade and the Charge of the Light Brigade. The glittering squadrons of light cavalry who had left England's shores in early 1854 with optimism and the expectation that their superiority in battle would see a swift end to hostilities had in effect ceased to exist such was the extent of its losses of both horses and men. Added to this was one of the coldest and cruellest winters ever known in the Crimea, something that highlighted the general mismanagement of the British commanders to the full and decimated the army still further. Russell's reports caused a national outcry which led to the falling of Lord Aberdeen's government in early 1855. Aberdeen was not the only high- profile casualty: after seeing his army perish over the winter the Commander-in-Chief himself, Lord Raglan, died a broken man in June 1855 of 'Crimea Fever'.

As it turned out, Isaac was a member of the last group of inexperienced recruits given orders to prepare for action. On 2nd September 1855, under the command of Cornet Henry Marshall, he and his fellow troopers embarked and prepared to sail for the Crimea the following day.

Although the last conventional battle in the Crimea took place at Inkerman in November 1854, the long siege of Sevastopol prolonged the war for another eighteen months. As the Russians dug in, the British Cavalry were virtually redundant. This all occurred while the young reinforcements under Cornet Marshall's command were at sea. Private Scott and his colleagues were destined to see no action but as the war would not be ended until April 1856, the group of young soldiers were entitled to, and later duly received, their Crimean campaign medal along with the clasp for Sevastopol and the Turkish Sultan's Medal, awarded to each member of the allied forces for the armed struggle in defence of the Turkish Empire. Isaac, therefore, was one of the non-combatants whose medal award so infuriated Jacob Reed and his colleagues.

The long sea journey commenced on 3rd September 1855 and retraced the trip made by the allied forces over twelve months earlier, ending with a landing in Kalamita Bay on 24th September. Frustratingly for the young Private Scott, he arrived to find the war all but over, although he did enter the fortress of Sevastopol with the rest of his regiment upon their arrival.

Isaac was the last of many soldiers who bolstered the British forces during 1855. By the middle of November he had helped strengthen the 17th Lancers, which now totalled 15 officers and 291 non-commissioned officers and men with 224 horses; a dramatic improvement on the paltry numbers at the beginning of the year. If he was in any doubt about the type of fighting he had missed during the campaign to date, or that which he was likely to encounter later in his career, he was brought up to speed when listening to the stories of his new-found colleagues: men like Privates James Wightman and John Veigh who had both participated in the Charge of the Light Brigade, and witnessed their colleagues and horses wiped out by disease during the following winter, as they struggled on with poor facilities and inadequate equipment. John Veigh, the regimental butcher, was a particularly interesting character. 'Butcher Jack', as his colleagues called him, was partial to the odd scam and was renowned for overstepping the mark from time to time. On the night before 'the charge' he had been separated from his colleagues for being drunk on duty. On the morning of 25th October, hearing his regiment were about to charge the Russian guns, he rushed to rejoin them and charged down the valley in his bloodstained canvas smock, carrying his pole-axe instead of a lance!

Thankfully the commanding officers, having learned from the catastrophic experience of the previous winter, decided that the retention of the cavalry in the Crimea would be futile and would also increase the risk of unnecessary loss of man and beast. The decision was therefore made to move them away from the area for the impending winter. The 17th embarked in two transports, the *Candia* and the *Etna*, along with the 13 other cavalry regiments at Balaclava Harbour.

Most of the regiments set sail for Scutari, where they wintered. Three regiments, however, known as 'The Hussar Brigade' and consisting of the 17th Lancers, the 8th Hussars and the 10th Hussars, were sent further south east on a four-day sea journey to another Turkish port, Ismid, under the command of Brigadier Shewell. They remained there until the proclamation of peace at the Treaty of Paris on 27th April 1856. The likelihood is that Isaac's parents probably knew of the treaty before the news was carried across the continent to their son in the field. The *Penrith Herald* reported, with some bitterness, two days after peace had been declared:

> [...] *this madness has finally come to an end with the signing of the treaty. But what is the cost? The feeling of ardent patriotism that inspired so many to fight has resulted in human sacrifices of incalculable proportion. The effect on the British Empire is ambivalent. Let us now hope for peace; never again must our young men be forced to give their lives for a cause they know little of.*

In fact, a degree of stability in Eastern Europe had been maintained. But the editor of the *Herald* was right to point out the cost: through fighting and illness the war claimed the lives of 22,000 British soldiers, almost as many as had been sent out in the original army. It proved to be France's only successful military campaign of the nineteenth century but at a cost of between 50,000 and 100,000 French lives. The war also accounted for the lives of half a million Russians — Tsar Nicholas himself, the chief architect of the war, died of pneumonia in March 1855 — and bankrupted both the Russian and Ottoman Empires, with the latter seeing the weakening of its already fragile hold on many of its member states. This erosion in itself would lead to constant, seemingly endless armed conflict between neighbouring states; conflict that has never been resolved in the 150 years since the end of the war.

On 29th April 1856, a no-doubt somewhat crestfallen Private Scott, not having seen any action, and his colleagues boarded the *Candia*, bound for home. Arriving at Queenstown, Ireland, on 14th May, the regiment quartered at Cahir barracks, where the depot squadron, who had remained at their home base in Brighton throughout the conflict, joined it. It also had detachments at Clogheen, Clonmel, Fethard and Limerick.

A relatively quiet twelve-month peacekeeping period then followed for the 17th Lancers, in an Ireland whose belly was still growling due to the famine-ridden years of the 1840s. If life was tough for the soldiers, it was incomprehensible for the people of Ireland, a large percentage of whom lived on the open plains, in huts made of sods of the soft, elastic turf and gorse.

Such postings may well have been peaceful for the army, but they were not without hazards and risks to its men. Large garrisons, both in Ireland and on the mainland, invariably attracted prostitutes. The 'wrens' as they were known in Ireland, were known to give birth on the plain and raise their offspring while continuing to ply their trade in order to feed and clothe themselves and their children. This inescapable downward spiral of depravity and disease reduced life expectancy among such women to an incredible twenty-five. (The authority's wider battle against prostitution reached its zenith in the 1840s. It would have you believe that it was seeking to stamp out such immorality for the good of society, but in truth its high-principled stance happily coincided with its own best interests. Whilst patrolling the moral high ground, it was discovered that venereal disease was a major drain on the army's manpower. On a single day in 1844, one regiment found over a quarter of its men to be infected with either syphilis or gonorrhœa.)

The only (other) thing that broke the monotony of barrack-room life for the men of the 17th was the moving of the regiment en masse to different barracks during the period: to Portobello Barracks in Dublin on 12th September 1856, and to Island Bridge Barracks, across town, on 7th March 1857.

On 15th September 1857, whilst parading for evening stables, the regiment was issued with an order to hold themselves in readiness to proceed to Queenstown and there embark for another foreign campaign. The men spontaneously broke into cheering, sending their stable bags and caps flying into the air with delight at the prospect of ending their peacetime frustration and being given the chance of serving their Queen in another distant corner of her Empire. The object of the campaign was to suppress the mutiny in India, details of which had filtered through to the British Isles throughout the summer of 1857.

The 17th had stood ready for the call to arms all summer long, frustrated at the interminable delay, knowing that the Indian insurrection had occurred some four months earlier. Finally their time had arrived; finally Isaac was to see some action. On 1st October the depot was formed, and on the 6th the regiment prepared for transportation by rail from Dublin to Cork. Standing at ten troops they consisted of 504 officers and men.

James Wightman, now promoted to sergeant, described the classic Victorian military scene in his diary:

> It was a grand sight to see our fellows full of vigour on their way to the station which was lined with people cheering and admiring their round and jolly faces — willingly going to battle, wives crying, girls rushing in the our midst to kiss their sweethearts and even children running along with us. The procession formed an imposing spectacle and nothing could equal the popular enthusiasm.

Upon their arrival at Cork they joined their colleagues from the Crimea, the 8th Hussars, and took the river steamers at St Patrick's Bridge prior to boarding the *Great Britain* under the command of Captain Grey. Two days later the steamship weighed anchor and set out for India. While the lads on board gave three cheers, the onlookers on the dockside waved and shouted their approval, and a band played them off with *The Girl I Left Behind Me*.

The 42-day journey to Cape Town passed uneventfully, but upon reaching the tip of South Africa, where the ship stopped for coal, the spirits of the men sank at hearing that Delhi had been retaken from the rebels. The feeling pervaded the decks of Captain Grey's ship that the Mutiny would have been suppressed before they reached India. What must Isaac have thought as he climbed into his hammock that November night? History appeared to be repeating itself as far as he was concerned: having arrived in the Crimea too late, he seemed destined to have the same thing happen in India. Is this what he joined the army for: to be sent half a world away on campaigns, only to arrive after the main event?

✳ ✳ 4 ✳ ✳

The *Great Britain* arrived in Bombay on 17th December. Isaac's regiment had a pretty inauspicious start to the campaign: at the sight of the Indian port, the men on board surged forward and one fell overboard. Fortunately he was rescued; fortunately for him and fortunately for a relieved Captain Grey, who announced to his passengers that had the man been lost it would mean 'one hundred pounds out of my pocket!'

The 17th disembarked in two divisions, the first on 19th December and the second, containing Private Scott, on 21st December. Both divisions were moved to Kirkee, about 75 miles south east of Bombay, arriving on 24th and 26th December respectively. There then followed a period of further frustration for the regiment, as with their arrival at Kirkee came the weariness of inactivity, which was compounded by the uncertainty of the current strategic situation elsewhere in the country, and not least the fact that they had very few horses at their disposal.

During their journey to the subcontinent, Tantia Topi, one of the ringmasters of the rebellion, had split up from his leader, Nana Sahib, after the British had regained control of Delhi and Cawnpore. In doing so Nana entrusted Tantia with commanding the 'Gwalior Contingent' of the rebel army. The British were aware that if they could capture these two main protagonists, it would see an end to the uprising.

Tantia had been joined by Roa Sahib, Nana's nephew, and with an army of 25,000 had briefly retaken Cawnpore in November 1857 only to be defeated and routed by Sir Colin Campbell a month later. (This was one of the actions Private Jacob Reed and the Rifle Brigade had participated in.) Tantia then turned north and captured the town of Chirkaree and then the fortress at Gwalior itself, prior to being defeated by Sir Hugh Rose in June 1858. Still undismayed Tantia broke away in a westerly direction to Tonk and by doing so triggered a ten-month cat and mouse game with the British around Central India.

The situation in Central India was highly complex because the region was divided into some 150 princely states, spanning six kingdoms. While the British had to pick their way carefully round the country, identifying who was loyal and who was not before progressing, Tantia, with his local knowledge and network of spies, could recruit at will and arrange food and horses to be readied for him as he passed through the appropriate districts.

Extra Arab horses arrived at Kirkee on 18th May and as they did the 17th were gradually sent to aid Sir Hugh Rose in the pursuit of Tantia. As more horses were brought in, each squadron was mounted and sent to the chase. The first was dispatched to Mhow, in late May, a 500-mile march that took three days. Hitherto, the 17th had seen no action and their immaculate uniforms caught the attention of officers from other regiments who commented on how smart they looked as they joined the pursuit. It would not be long, however, before the conditions in which they were working took their toll on men, horses and equipment. (May 1858 was one of the worst months of the whole campaign for the Europeans. More than a thousand British soldiers died of sunstroke, fatigue and disease, while about a hundred were killed in action).

Like his newly arrived Arabian horse, Private Scott was champing at the bit by this time; his squadron, however, were not destined to leave Kirkee for another frustrating month. Weather conditions were appalling: when the heavy rains were not soaking them, the Europeans were scorched by the burning sun. On one occasion the recorded heat in the Medical Officer's double roofed tent was 115° Fahrenheit. Lieutenant James Boys wrote in his diary:

> *During the whole day we were nearly suffocated by a terrible hot wind. These suffocating winds like a blast of the sirocco tell terribly on our poor fellows. Morale is low as none of us know which is best, engaging with the enemy and all the risks that entails, or being locked up in this intolerable inertia.*

It was early August before this detachment could rejoin their colleagues and, under the command of Major White, march to Sholapur, 220 miles south east of Bombay, in an effort to anticipate Tantia's route. The guerrilla leader, however, continued to lead his chasers a merry dance as he headed north to Jhalra-Patan where he boosted his rebel army with the Rajah's 10,000 mutineers and gained possession of 40 cannons as well as a considerable treasure. The British soldiers' depression at losing their prey was compounded by the heavy monsoon rains: the wet, the muggy heat and the mosquitoes combined to drain the spirits from the hardiest of combatants. As any old India-hand will tell you, nothing ever gets dry during the rains; gear and weapons rust; clothes rot and wounds don't heal. Under such conditions did the game of cat and mouse continue as the mutineers headed for Indore, where they were cut off by two British columns and retreated to Rajghur. This signalled Tantia's last offensive movement; from now on, he was to lead his mutineers through the dense jungles of Central India hotly pursued by the British.

September saw a 1,100-strong British force comprising elements of five regiments under the command of General Michel march from north of

17th Lancers on parade at Secunderabad, India, c1863
(Queen's Royal Lancers Museum)

Mhow to Rajghur to meet the rebels. Conditions worsened after heavy rains had turned the Indian cotton soil into a sea of black mud. The march took eleven hours to complete and when the sepoys were found, the British discovered an 800-strong army drawn up for battle in two lines. Even though the insurgents were set for combat they suspected British reinforcements were not far away and fled after a relatively minor skirmish into the Seronge Jungle. As this was happening, Private Scott's squadron were moved up to Mhow to support the advancing columns. What greeted him and his colleagues at Mhow was a cantonment under a burning sun that was covered in flies and foul smells from bodies in various stages of decomposition, owing to them not being buried deep enough.

Tantia, if not caught by this time, was certainly wriggling on the line. Splitting his rebel army in two with his lieutenant Roa Sahib in an attempt to disrupt the Europeans' pursuit proved unsuccessful, as further skirmishes in and around the jungle reduced numbers still further, and the two joined forces again within a month. In desperation he turned back across the Nerbuddha River and fled eastward into the Banswarra Jungle. This was the point where the British commanders felt they had their quarry. Although the guerrilla army remained high in numbers it was becoming increasingly disorganised.

It was now early December 1858. The 17th joined as one under the command of Colonel Benson and moved toward the jungle where the rebels were hiding. There followed a series of marches that would see the regiment cover more than a thousand miles in and around the vast dense undergrowth of Central India's jungles, in the chase for the rebel leader and his followers. Christmas Eve saw them march 17 miles from Ninose to Nowgaum on the north side of the jungle. Tantia emerged from the jungle on Christmas Day and, after a brief exchange of fire, with a small detachment of troops marched eastwards for Zeerapore.

Reconnaissance on the same day (the 25th) informed the British that the rebels had appeared and were heading for Mundesoor. The regiment therefore were forced into another long 36-mile march that took them most of the day. On their arrival they found the enemy encamped only four miles from their position. The mutineers then stole a march on the British by raising camp early and making their escape.

On the 27th they marched at daybreak, crossing the River Chumbul and catching up with the mutineers again who were encamped close by. The British bivouacked in sight of the rebel campfires and prepared to attack the following day. Rising at four o'clock, however, the British found only the smouldering fires of the enemy camp. The main body of rebels had retreated still further, and the pursuit was taken up again for a further 28 miles across the Kollee Sind River.

Wednesday 29th December saw a three o'clock call for Scott and his colleagues, marching from the right bank of the river for a further eight miles to reach sight of the rebel camp. Advancing over ploughed land so as to make as little noise as possible, the lancers waited for daylight before making their attack. Even then, Tantia and his rebel army showed great cunning: retreating a further two miles they drew themselves up into battle formation on rising ground with a deep ravine and dense jungle to their rear and waited for the 17th to emerge from the wooded lane opposite. Upon the appearance of their enemy the sepoys opened fire. Colonel Benson split his regiment into columns of divisions to counter. Sending his leading column to attack the right flank also allowed his guns to open fire with grape and shell at a distance of 400 yards. The regiment magnificently executed this, and the rebels soon scattered and were driven into the jungle. The 17th saw their opportunity to rout the mutineers and immediately took up the chase once more, crossing the ravine and entering the jungle. They quickly found the rebels had regrouped and drawn up in a new position but their futile counter-attack came to nothing and again they retreated into the undergrowth, with the thundering horses of the British Cavalry at their heels.

The running battle between the 17th Lancers and Tantia's increasingly diminishing army continued for two hours, covering a staggering 36 miles.

At its conclusion the insurgents had been scattered and seven of the rebel leader's elephants (laden with bags containing gold bricks), as well as a supply of arms had been captured. Defiantly, however, Tantia himself remained at large. Not renowned for his anger-management skills and effective leadership techniques, in a fit of rage at the loss of his guns and treasure, he promptly shot one of his own chief officers dead!

The distance covered by the soldiers in pursuit of their target had been 178 miles, including the crossing of two large rivers with heavy cannon, in six days. This is all the more remarkable when it is considered that they were without European supplies and as a result had no protection from the hot days and the bitterly cold nights. Through all of this, the regiment had only one man wounded and two horses killed.

But still there was no respite for the soldiers as on 30th December the relentless pursuit continued and the rebels were engaged once more at Zeerapore. The guerrillas' continuing determination was demonstrated here, as the British were fired on as they approached the rebel site and, although not driven back, had to halt their advance and camp for the night. In spite of the atrocious muddy conditions, exhausted troopers, bridle in hand, were asleep in minutes where they dismounted.

There was another daybreak awakening for the British soldiers on 31st December, another advance, only to find a further example of the rebels' fortitude, as they had moved off the night before, resulting in a seven-mile march for the regiment towards Baroda.

The first day of 1859 witnessed the Battle of Baroda. After brief exchanges of gunfire, two columns of lancers were drawn up and charged the rebel positions, scattering their target as they approached. Plunging headlong among them they kept up the slaughter for seven miles, capturing all of Tantia's Zomboruks (small cannons mounted on camels' backs) with every lance and sword seeing action until men and horses alike were worn out. Remarkable courage and stamina was shown here again by man and beast alike: fewer than 100 cavalrymen took on this force of over 3,000, albeit disorganised, enemy, with the only casualty to themselves during the day's pursuit being one soldier wounded .

Private Isaac Scott was one of these 100 men and this was to remain his most significant action during his military career. At last he was experiencing the adventure he had volunteered for three years earlier. Two of Scott's colleagues to charge that day was were Private John Brown and Lieutenant H. E. Wood, both of whom would go on to command the regiment in the late nineteenth century. The chase was not only in itself a tremendous achievement for those taking part and the regiment, but the

Battle of Baroda proved a mortal blow for Tantia and his army.

Scott, Brown, Wood and the rest of the two columns who set up the victory were worn out after the long running battle. Their reward for such a successful pursuit? Further exposure to the cruel subcontinental weather conditions as, in a cruel climax to the day, torrential rain fell on a bitterly cold night forcing the men and their charges, without supplies, once more to sleep in fetlock-deep mud. One rider's vivid description leaves nothing to the imagination:

> There is nothing more uncomfortable than riding in the rain. You can never get warm — cold rain soaks your tunic to your body so the chill mingles with your sweat and seeps down into your bones. Your muscles seize up and grow heavy with frigid, sodden exhaustion.

Sheer fatigue from the day's events, however, forced sleep on them, and their colleagues who had camped at the village joined them the following day. Thus the 17th Lancers were joined as one again and together they pushed on with even greater zeal, sensing the rebels were there for the taking. The regiment's relentless chase over the vast distances and treacherous terrain continued, but developed into more of a mopping-up exercise as pockets of guerrillas were rounded up on a regular basis. A further 54 and 40 miles respectively were covered in two circular marches in as many days.

The soldiers finally enjoyed some comfort after four days' halt at Baroda and then moved in a northwesterly direction to Chuppra, where a baggage column rejoined them on 9th January, to their great comfort; Sergeant Wightman recorded that they had not had a change of underclothing since Christmas Day. As these supply visits were desperately infrequent and the regiment, far removed from its commissariat, had to be self sufficient, it is fair to assume that Isaac and colleagues with a similar civilian trade, would have acted as regimental tailors to their colleagues in the field, fixing and mending as best they could.

The men's comfort was fleeting, however, as they were forced, under the incessant taunting of chattering monkeys and chirruping birds, to pick their way along the floor of the Seronge Jungle, through the dense undergrowth, for a further 256 miles over the next eight days. They engaged and defeated Tantia twice during this period (on 16th and 21st January) but this would come at a price for Private Scott. It was during one of these clashes that Scott was advancing in skirmishing order and firing whilst mounted, as was the custom. During the encounter, he received a gunshot wound to the right calf. The bullet entered his leg, causing damage to nerves and the gastrocnemius muscle as well as grazing the tibia bone, and although it was by no means a life-threatening injury, it was enough to see him carried from the vanguard of the action and back to Baroda for several weeks.

Being young and fit, receiving medical supervision, and being allowed to rest, Isaac's recovery from the wound was a relative formality. The nagging injury would, however, prove a permanent weakness and cause particular discomfort in later life.

Although they were just about keeping their pursuers at bay, the feeling of inevitable defeat continued to permeate through the rebel ranks at this time as further evidence of uncertainty and infighting came to light. Two of Tantia's lieutenants split from their leader and disappeared into the Banswarra Jungle only to be defeated and captured on 10th February. This left Tantia and his decimated force to scatter and hide in the neighbouring Paron Jungle.

While the regiment waited in their camp on the edge of the tropical labyrinth, they held a ceremony on Wednesday 23rd February at which a Victoria Cross was presented to one of their number, Regimental Sergeant Major Woodin, for his distinguished conduct at the Battle of Balaclava and his rescuing of Captain Morris during the famous charge. The timing of such a ceremony may seem strange to us today (why not wait for some investiture at the Palace?) but they were held purely for expediency. The life expectancy of soldiers abroad at this time was greatly reduced, due to both combat and disease. If awards were not dished out as soon as possible, the poor recipients might not live long enough to receive them!

Fragmenting daily, Tantia's force was now reduced to 500 rebels and they knew that whatever action they took was simply delaying the inevitable. Sergeant Wightman again described how his NCO colleague, Sergeant Greaves killed Tantia's lieutenant, Roa Sahib. Interestingly he wrote, 'Sergeant Greaves dismounted and looted his body and saddlebags and found some saleable jewellery.' It is clear from this testimony that the British soldiers (as during Wellington's period) were still allowed to enjoy such spoils of war.

✳ ✳ 5 ✳ ✳

In early March 1859 the *Penrith Observer* reported the surrender by 300 mutineers to their incessant pursuers at Mottapoora in Central India. Probably unknown to them at the time, this was one of the few snippets of information William and Agness Scott had about their son's exploits during the Central India campaign. Whereas William Howard Russell's reports from the north of the country, where he was accompanying Sir Colin Campbell in his chase for Nana Sahib, continued to filter through *The Times* and into the provincial newspapers, the chase over thousands of miles for the other Mutiny warlord, Tantia Topi, was such that regular updates were virtually impossible to communicate to the outside world.

Despite the surrendering of the 300, Tantia, who had shown genius for guerrilla warfare during the uprising and had engaged the British in battle on no fewer than sixteen occasions, remained on the run throughout the jungle for a further month until Rajah Maun Singh betrayed him to the British.

Maun Singh was a vassal of Scindia and had quarrelled with Tantia some time prior to the Mutiny. When the Raja refused to join Tantia's army at the height of the uprising, the latter imprisoned him. In so doing, Tantia ignored the age-old proverb, 'Be nice to people on the way up, as you may need them on the way back down,' for Maun Singh escaped his subjugator the following year. When Tantia returned and sought asylum in the Rajah's territory, he initially agreed but after some deliberation betrayed his countryman to the British. Had Maun Singh not turned whistle-blower, it is questionable as to whether the rebel leader would have ever been caught.

Accompanied by two cooks and his groom, Tantia was surrounded by British soldiers while still asleep on the morning of 7th April 1859. After being roused by his captors, he is reported to have asked Maun Singh, "What friendship is this?"

"I never considered you as a friend," the Rajah replied coldly.

For the British, the last major objective had been realised. In terms of time, it took longer to suppress the rebellion in Central India than in any other region. From 22nd June 1858 (Isaac's 24th birthday) till 7th April 1859 the British forces had pursued Tantia Topi all over the centre of the country, Rajputana and Berar — the widest area in terms of length and breadth when compared to all the other campaigns during the two- year conflict. The pursuit, though militarily insignificant because nothing strategic was at stake (more a matter of principle that such a figure should be caught) was an inspiring part of the rebellion. During this episode, Tantia Topi laid the foundations for modern guerrilla warfare in the jungles of Central India.

Once in custody, he was taken to Sipri where no time was lost in charging him with rebellion. "I only obeyed my master's orders," he said in his defence at his trial. "I have nothing to do with the murder of any European men, women or children" — a reference to the Cawnpore massacre. The court did not believe him and he was sentenced to hang.

Private Scott was back with the main body of his regiment by this time and given their relentless pursuit of the rebel leader the 17th Lancers were ordered to attend Tantia's execution. On the morning of 18th April, Scott and his mounted colleagues stood in silent parade order on the dusty courtyard of the cantonment at Sipri. It was another sweltering day and a hot wind blew across the dusty parade ground. The only movement came from the horses: a tail swishing the flies away, or a head jerking down and forward as it restlessly pulled on its bit and bridle. At the far end of the courtyard, a large double door opened and a bedraggled figure, flanked by his gaolers, was escorted through. He walked the fifty paces to the scaffold, passing his captors who looked down with on him with contempt.

Lieutenant Wood later wrote,

> To Tantia, acting under Nana Sahib, had been attributed the arrangements of the treacherous slaughter of Sir Hugh Wheeler's force at Cawnpore. This was put to him as he stood on the gallows, but the snivelling wretch denied it.

He went on to describe his hanging: a 'painful one' (is there another type?) 'as his executioners were without experience.' One of those executioners was the Regiment's Farrier-Sergeant and he took the rope used as a souvenir (this sits in the regimental museum today as a macabre trophy, alongside the ornaments taken from Tantia's elephants the previous December.) Wood concluded with his feelings towards the rebel leader, describing him as 'neither well-born, rich nor brave, but clever and unscrupulous.' Sergeant Wightman was equally scathing in his diary: 'Tantia was at all times the first to leave the field,' he wrote, 'fleeing and leaving his defeated hordes behind him.' With Tantia's execution the dying embers of the Indian Mutiny were extinguished.

After the execution, Private Scott and his colleagues were ordered to the devastated cantonment at Morar, four miles to the east of Gwalior City and 200 miles south of Delhi, with a view to quelling possible further rebellion perpetrated by European members of the Indian Army.

With the disbandment of the East India Company, members of the Company's army were forced to transfer into the Queen's army. Company officers and soldiers challenged the validity of this transfer by arguing that it contravened the terms of their enlistment and the oath of allegiance the men had sworn on attestation: they had sworn allegiance to the Queen only as subjects and not as soldiers. The first evidence of such dissension occurred in Calcutta at the celebration of the transference of India to the Crown on the first day of November 1858, while Isaac was chasing Tantia around Central India. Roman candles and rockets were ignited on huge bamboo scaffolding. The fireworks went awry however, and an illumination of Queen Victoria caught fire, unintentionally burning her effigy. This caused great amusement amongst some disloyal natives and European members of the Company Army. They realized that from this day forward the Anglo-Native regiments ceased to be part of the East India Company and were to become part of Her Majesty's Indian Forces.

Notwithstanding the previous 18 months of savage warfare with mutinying Asian colleagues, British members of the Indian Army still challenged the legitimacy of their being subsumed by the Queen's army. Within a fortnight of the declaration, official protests were taking place. Whereas their nationality was not in question, paradoxically their loyalty to its armed forces was.

Lord Canning, Governor of India, sat back and hoped that the protests would evaporate, but as Tantia Topi was being chased round the jungles of Central India the rumblings of discontent amongst the European members of the former Bengal Army continued. This discontent gradually developed into further mutinous plotting, which was to culminate in a second uprising amongst the European members of the former Company army in Bengal. The mutiny itself was organized and commenced as planned on 10th May 1859, the second anniversary of the sepoys' rebellion. The epicentre of the rebellion was also the same: Meerut.

This largely unreported episode became known as the 'White Mutiny'. The protest remains the largest and most successful challenge to authority the British Army has ever experienced. The series of events leading up to and including the mutiny itself reveal the abiding tensions and ambivalence that existed between the Company army's officers and their counterparts in the Queen's army.

The 17th Lancers arrived at Morar and set up their regimental headquarters there, with a detachment at Jhansi, and were present to police the trials of the ringleaders of the mutiny that took place there during the summer months of 1859. The first trial to take place did so at dawn on 18th May, when members of the 3rd European Bengal Regiment were tried for their part in the uprising of 10th May. Results and sentencing varied between disbandments of regiments, deportation to Australia and in extreme cases, execution by firing squad.

Discontent was compounded amongst soldiers who did transfer from the Company's army to the Queen's army when they discovered they were not allowed to discharge. Some order was restored however when finally on 20th June Canning rescinded this mandate. This went some way to placating the former Indian Army members and incredibly, almost 10,000 from the Bengal Army alone took advantage of the privilege. In effect the British in India had yielded to intimidation: the mutineers had gained a victory and the British had been beaten by Europeans within the Indian Army after their successful struggle against the Asian contingent of the same army.

Canning felt secure enough to declare 'a state of peace' throughout India on 8th July 1859, and Isaac and his colleagues took part in a medal ceremony that saw the men of the 17th Lancers presented with their honours from the campaign; this included Lieutenant Wood receiving a Victoria Cross for his bravery during the pursuit of Tantia. Private Scott was awarded his Indian Mutiny campaign medal with his citation reading: 'For being engaged in the suppression of the Mutiny in Malwa and Central India during part of years 1858 and 1859.' As well as memorials to the dead at Cawnpore and Lucknow, as an act of conciliation memorials were also eventually erected to the Rani of Jhansi and Tantia Topi at Gwalior and Guna respectively.

Although with the capturing of Tantia the regiment had seen their last action in India, for the next twelve months the 17th Lancers were to encounter that silent yet ruthless old foe last experienced in the Crimea: cholera. Many officers and men were to lose their lives during the remaining months of 1859 as the indiscriminate killer took hold and ran through the regiment like a flame.

The transference of India from the East India Company to the Crown virtually ceased the governor's absolute executive power. Charles Canning, the Governor of India at the time, was given the title of Viceroy instead. (Canning was an unsung hero of the Mutiny; despite being criticised in both India and England he maintained a philosophy throughout of justice, not vengeance.) The East India Company thus lost its function and was abolished. The physical as well as mental scars littered the country in the aftermath of the war. By June 1858 Cawnpore remained desolate and in ruins and remained so for some years. In 1860, cholera plagued the city and soldiers were not allowed to venture there.

Post Mutiny reforms included a reduction in the number of Christian missionaries; their funds were also cut and their activities drastically restricted. Bible classes were abolished and forbidden in government schools. The British were by this time less concerned with converting the Indians and more with making certain that they were not provoked into another mutiny. Lord and Lady Canning commissioned a memorial at Cawnpore (neither of them would live to see it completed in 1865) and an enormous Romanesque church called All Souls was built near the Entrenchment in 1862. Despite the enormous number of Christians who lost their lives during the Mutiny, they were not put off from travelling to India, as the number of over 3,000 present in 1860 was double that of 1851. The cross over the well in Cawnpore where the dismembered bodies of the women and children lay became India's most hallowed shrine, receiving more visitors in the ten years after the Mutiny than the Taj Mahal.

Railway construction, postal and telegraph services and road building not only brought great benefits to the country but also strengthened the position of the British. In the event of any trouble information could be passed on instantly by telegraphic means, troops could be sent rapidly by train and any rebellion swiftly crushed.

For all the figurative and literal bridge building attempted by many in the years after the insurrection however, India remained far from stable. The resentment felt by locals towards Britain continued. Frequent disastrous famines, beginning with the 1866 Orissa famine, which took the lives of 1.5 million people, contributed substantially to political unrest. (Undeterred by this however, Benjamin Disraeli's government in 1876 would proclaim Queen Victoria Empress of India.)

There was also a requirement hastily to reform the post-Mutiny Indian

Army (or as it was now, the Indian arm of the British Army). The ratio of European troops to sepoys—who were an integral part of the peasant society who had followed them into revolt—was therefore increased. (This civil rebellion would never have taken place had not the military uprising sparked it off on that stifling Meerut evening in May 1857. At the time, the ratio of indigenous troops to their European counterparts was 5:1. From 1859 it was 2:1.)

But by increasing the ratio, the British suffered a self-inflicted double whammy. Not only did they need to replace native soldiers in the army, but the numbers problem was exacerbated by the high figure of European men who discharged themselves upon being transferred into the British Army after Canning's June concession. It was clear that several regiments were required to stay behind in India. Private Scott's 17th were one such regiment; so as Jacob Reed and his Rifle Brigade were setting off back to England, Isaac was preparing for the duration in India.

On the 10th January 1860 the 17th Lancers were ordered south to Secunderabad under the command of Major White. As the regiment was still tormented by the killer disease, the journey was to become known as 'The Cholera March'. The symptoms of cholera are diarrhoea and loss of water and salts, vomiting, thirst and muscle cramps. Death can occur as quickly as a few hours after the onset of symptoms, with the mortality rate being more than 50 per cent in untreated cases. This rate can be reduced to less than 1 per cent, however, with effective treatment. Given these statistics it is not surprising that a further 38 men were lost on the long march south.

Amongst the victims (and his story is a typical example of the indiscriminate cruelty of the disease) was Private John Veigh, the regimental butcher. It was another searingly hot day when the troopers halted to perform the daily, soul-destroying task of digging graves for their unfortunate colleagues who had fallen to the disease that particular day. Flocks of screeching kites, circling quietly overhead, witnessed the scene that was played out below them. As usual, the caravan was engulfed by the usual infestation of flies and 'Butcher Jack' was digging one of the graves when he was overcome by a fit of uncontrollable coughing; droplets of blood preceded the telltale signs of retching; his desperate pleading to his colleagues for water was as futile as their efforts to satisfy his needs. He died within hours and was buried in the very grave he had been digging for another of his anguished colleagues. Thus ended the life of this brave character who had been present for the duration of the Crimean War; who had travelled home to Ireland with his regiment prior to accompanying them to the subcontinent; chasing his enemy around the jungles of Central

India and seeing an end to hostilities, only to die from cholera on a remote road, thousands of miles from home in the middle of nowhere.

His beleaguered colleagues arrived at Secunderabad, just north of Hyderabad, in late March 1860. Upon their arrival the 17th made Secunderabad their regimental headquarters and remained there in a relatively quiet period for almost five years. In 1861 Major Robert White, who had distinguished himself throughout the campaign and taken the regiment to Secunderabad, became Lieutenant Colonel. Reduced to staying fit and maintaining a state of readiness by training and taking long marches, the regiment saw no further action during this period; mutiny had been replaced by monotony. The soldier's day began and ended with bugle and roll calls. His year proceeded through an established cycle: the daily pay parade and rum ration, the monthly accounting or muster day, the annual brigade and divisional inspections, clothing issue or regimental anniversary.

The extreme meteorological cycles of the country dictated human activity. From April to June summer heat imprisoned the men in barracks in sweaty, irritated indolence. The barrack-rooms could be unbearably hot, although the troopers of the 1860s did have some advantage over some of their predecessors as punkahs were installed into the barrack-rooms in 1850. This was only light relief, however, as most free time was spent lying on their cots on stifling summer days. The change in the weather saw further problems: the monsoon, arriving in July and at first welcomed, brought cholera and fevers. The only respite for the men from the tedium of camp life came through the leisure activities they arranged between themselves: horse or pony races, polo and pig sticking.

For the soldiers stationed in the far corners of the Empire the only contact they had with their homeland was through the long (nine weeks in India's case) sea voyage that carried letters to and from their base. It was one such letter from his father in early 1864 that brought heart-wrenching news to the trooper from Cumberland. He learned that the woman he had left behind, his mother Agness, had died on 25th November 1863.

What would Isaac be thinking at this point: as a soldier, as a son? It must surely have been the lowest ebb of his career; with his wound causing discomfort, the uncomfortable tropical conditions of India, the relative inactivity of the peacetime soldier and now the terrible news from England that must have brought pangs of guilt when he recalled how his mother tried to dissuade him from joining the army. This was the beginning of an unsettling period for him, one that was resolved to a certain degree by the decision to recall the 17th Lancers to England and so end their unbroken eight years' service in India. On 14th December 1864 the regiment left Secunderabad for the last time. A 16-day march took them to Sholapore before travelling by train to Poona where they remained until 20th January 1865. The 17th embarked on the *Agamemnon* on the 21st at Bombay and sailed for home.

Victorian military campaigns were renowned for not only pitting the wits of the British soldier against his enemy but also placing him at the disadvantage of doing so amid inhospitable conditions totally alien to him. The experiences of the 17th Lancers were no different during their stay in India. The regiment had recruited a total number of 48 officers and 404 men but suffered incredible losses from climatic causes and disease. Deaths and invaliding, not to mention the number lost in battle, amounted to an extraordinary 38 officers and 373 men, over eighty per cent of the total that left Ireland in 1858.

✳ ✳ 7 ✳ ✳

April 1865 saw the 17th Lancers land at Tilbury and in so doing touch home soil for the first time in eight years. On 6th May they marched to their new Regimental Headquarters at Colchester, where they were to remain until March 1866. During the remaining months of 1865 the campaign-weary soldiers were given leave to visit their homes after being away for so long; in Private Scott's case he made the long journey north to Penrith during that summer.

Upon his arrival he was to find much had changed in his eleven-year absence. Cosmetic and architectural changes to the town included the building of the handsome Musgrave Monument and Clock Tower, erected in May 1861 in tribute to the eldest son of Sir George and Lady Musgrave who had died two years earlier. Another change to the centre of the town was the newly cobbled Corn Market that had been a hive of activity since Penrith's inception as a market town in the thirteenth century; this was an area of the town Isaac was very familiar with, having served his apprenticeship only yards away from the Corn Market on Angel Lane. The greatest change however was a personal one: the loss of his mother, the woman he had left behind ten years earlier with her protestations to his joining the army ringing in his ears. His widowed father, William, was still prospering at his town centre pub, the Grate Inn.

What sort of conversation took place between father and son after ten years apart? Their experiences in that period could not have been more contrasted: William had remained in the small Cumberland market town, witnessed his youngest son, Joseph, marry and move to the northeast, and suffered the personal pain and loss of his wife. Isaac on the other hand had witnessed barbarity on a unimaginable scale in an exotic land on the other side of the world—yet here they were, trying to pick up pieces and make amends for mistakes and regrets.

Whatever the topic of conversation, Isaac's visit home after so long proved unsettling; unsure about his future he returned to his regiment. For the Victorian soldier, used as he was to seemingly endless campaigns, peace service and barrack room life—whether in India, England or anywhere else for that matter—was a fairly mundane affair. It is true that the cavalryman was slightly better off than the foot soldier but both were modestly paid and therefore had little money to spend, and little to do. It is clear that Scott's enthusiasm for continued service was waning as many of his comrades from foreign fields left the regiment or retired upon their return. He marched with his regiment to their new headquarters at Aldershot in 1866 and saw his commanding officer and colleague from India, Colonel White, retire and be succeeded by Colonel Drury Lowe.

By the turn of the new year, 1867, Private Scott finally made up his mind to leave the army; on the morning of 15th April 1867, with his regiment still at Aldershot, he marched into his commanding officer's office for the last time — his service, time expired. Receiving a stiff handshake and 19s 2d from the Paymaster Lieutenant Stephenson, which included his train fair home, he returned to Penrith.

While happy to billet with his father, Isaac chose not to help with the running of William's tavern. Instead he took a job that appears to have been as far removed from the previous twelve years as could be imagined: he swapped the blue tunic, the mount and the state of readiness of a British cavalryman for the blue tunic, the mount and the rather more sedate profession of a rural postman. Working between 7am and 5pm, his duties not only included the servicing of the outlying areas but looking after the horses used for that purpose.

Appearing content to settle into the quiet east Cumberland lifestyle once more, Isaac nevertheless did not completely sever his ties with the military. Within months of his return he enlisted in the Westmorland and Cumberland Yeomanry, enrolling as a sergeant, which was customary given his military experience in the regular army. (The Yeomanry regiments had been in existence since 1794. They were conceived as a peacetime force, consisting of part-time volunteers, to guard against possible invasion from Revolutionary France when the regular army was abroad; this was as well as aiding Civil Power.)

The Westmorland and Cumberland Yeomanry were created in 1819, the same year the Manchester and Salford Yeormanry caused such havoc at the Peterloo Massacre. Far from decrying the yeomanry force, there is evidence in the local press that the Peterloo 'incident', as it was termed, served as a catalyst and inspiration for the forming of the Westmorland and Cumberland version. Instead of reporting the shambolic, tragic events as they happened, the *Carlisle Journal* rather praised the part-time force of Manchester for their 'gallant conduct' and described them as 'doughty and victorious heroes'.

Thus the local Yeomanry force, initially called the Westmorland Yeomanry, was formed on 22nd October 1819 with its commanding officer Hon Henry Cecil Lowther, the second son of the Earl of Lonsdale. 'Cumberland' was added to the title of the regiment in 1843, as there were three troops in each county: Edenhall, Dalemain and Milnthorpe in

Cumberland; and Appleby, Kendal and Shap (later Lowther) in Westmorland. The Lord Lieutenant made officer appointments, while the rank and file was made up of landholders and tenant farmers who provided their own mounts. The Government sponsored the Yeomanry Regiments by providing arms, swords, horse pistols and carbines. The former Private Scott of the 17th Lancers enrolled as Sergeant Scott of the Edenhall troop on 1st August 1867.

As the 19th century wore on, the Yeomanry regiments gradually attained credibility and respect and, along with the Volunteers (of whom we shall learn more later), they eventually proved to be an invaluable recruiting ground for the regular army. The latter half of the century saw radical changes in the reserve force that gradually evolved into the Territorial Army of the present day. Annual training camps for the whole regiment were held on a tented Foundry Field. Officers of the regular cavalry also carried out period parades and training inspections.

If the lancer uniform Scott had hung up earlier in the year had been modelled on the Polish Army, then the Yeomanry Hussar uniform his was now donning was derived from the Hungarian Horsemen of the seventeenth century. The Westmorland and Cumberland Regiment was one of the most resplendent of its type, with magnificent uniforms: scarlet dolman (short tunic), dark blue skin-tight overalls and black Hussar Busby. Sergeant Scott's duties included training of individuals throughout the year in basic manoeuvres, and in preparation for civil action. Other duties were ceremonial and would include escorting Royalty, officers of the law or even prisoners between one point and another.

It was not only Isaac but also the whole country that witnessed major change in that watershed year of 1867. The Reform Bill of that year was prompted by widespread dissatisfaction with the limited reforms of the 1832 Act. It created a number of new boroughs; decreased the parliamentary representation of boroughs with populations of fewer than 10,000; enlarged the representation of the counties; and broadened the electorate by decreasing financial qualifications and by enfranchising householders, mostly working men, in the boroughs. Isaac Scott, recently of the British Army, had the right to vote. And the major change to his life didn't end there: within twelve months of his homecoming, a chance encounter occurred that was to change his life. Jane Johnson was the daughter of blacksmith Thomas Johnson, who had his own shop on Friar's Street. She and the former soldier began courting; Jane, at 26, was seven years Isaac's junior.

The following year saw fate play a strange hand with the young couple.

Firstly, one warm spring morning there followed yet another example of how working-class Victorians, with inappropriate hygiene standards and make-do medical care, lived on a constant, unknowing, knife-edge between seemingly perfect health and sudden, indiscriminate death. Thomas, Jane's father, was hard at work in his forge; stripped to the waist and sweating profusely, he went out into the yard and doused himself down with cold water from the sluice pump, something he had done hundreds of times before. On this occasion, however, Thomas caught a chill from the extreme change in body temperature and was confined to bed. Whilst there, he contracted pneumonia and on the morning of 27th May 1868 the strapping blacksmith was pronounced dead.

Naturally upset by the loss, Jane and Isaac looked to rebuild their future and make it secure. In September Scott gave up his profession as a postman, as he decided to move temporarily to Liverpool, which was crying out for skilled and unskilled labour alike, due to the thriving shipbuilding industry. The Penrithian had scarcely been on the Mersey a month however, when his own father, William, died suddenly on 22nd October. Thus Isaac's future was settled and his financial position secured (albeit unsatisfactorily) as he returned home to inherited ownership of his father's inn. (His brother, Joseph, was a printer and lived and worked in the north-east.)

Due to his military history Isaac was by now a well-known figure in the town, and he settled happily into the running of the pub, something he was to continue doing for the next nine years. His happiness was complete when on 13th May 1869 he and Jane were married at St Andrew's Church. They celebrated the birth of their first child the following year, a daughter they named Amy Agness.

If this famous period in British history is divided into three, then the move from mid-Victorian to late-Victorian England is best placed at some point in the 1870s. But England's land was looking less green and decidedly unpleasant for many of Her Majesty's subjects, and the decade would prove to be one of doubt and uncertainty for many. The first sign of a change of direction and mood actually came in 1867 with the passing of the second Reform Act, which granted the vote to a substantial section of the urban working classes. In Westminster, there was uncertainty about what would be the outcome. Benjamin Disraeli, Peel's great opponent in the Parliamentary debates on the repeal of the Corn Laws, introduced the measure, but by the time that it passed so many amendments had been made that the Act bore little resemblance to the first Bill. Its passing was rightly regarded as a 'leap in the dark', and the first politician to benefit from it was the man who had emerged as Disraeli's great rival, the Liberal William Gladstone, who became Prime Minister the following year.

Gladstone and Disraeli, whose rivalry first surfaced in the 1850s when they clashed over the Corn Laws and the Indian Mutiny amongst other things, were temperamentally as well as politically completely different, and their rivalry was to last until Disraeli's death in 1881. While it lasted, the extended electorate was polarised; the two exchanged the keys of Number 10 on several occasions as the country battled through this unsettling period.

It was in late-Victorian England that the oft referred-to North-South divide in society became increasingly evident. Strong professional groups were established, and more occupations sought the reputable keeping-up-with-the-Joneses 'professional' status. With a strong City of London interest, and knowing that the strength of the world economy depended on a gold standard maintained by the privately-owned Bank of England, the language of politics became more strident than it had been in the middle years of the century.

The provinces, meanwhile, had to make their own arrangements. The 1860s had seen the end of the cotton industry in the north west; the 1870s were seeing a nationwide depression in agriculture as the home economy was starting to feel the pinch of competition from America and Europe, the main characteristic being its exports starting to take a sharp downturn. For the first time, there was a serious economic threat to aristocratic income. As a large share in the market was taken up by imports of food from abroad, rents began to fall, as did prices, and some land passed out of economic use. More competition may have been good for the consumer, but it was decidedly bad for the farmer: many went bankrupt, as they and their landowners did not share in the new age of plenty.

Although our publican and part-time soldier was not directly affected by this slump, Isaac Scott had inherited his father's business acumen and he recognised that he could potentially suffer, as some of his customers and the local economy felt the effects of the change. Change was also taking place in the Scott household itself; as the decade progressed, his family started to increase. His first son, Frank, was born three years after Amy, and Charles, Florence and Nelson would appear before the decade was out.

It was, of course, Queen Victoria herself who had set the trend in large families, producing nine children of her own, although strangely she did not care for babies. She admitted this frankly to her eldest daughter, Vicky, who was expecting her first at the time, in her remarkably candid letters when she compared them to cabbages! Vicky produced her mother's first grandchild in 1859 when her son, Wilhelm, was born on 27th January. The infant would grow up to make his own mark on history as Kaiser Wilhelm II of Germany.

By the time the tiny Scotts started to appear, however, such a family size was the exception rather than the rule. As the late-Victorian era began there was talk not of overpopulation but of underpopulation. During the 1870s there was a distinct fall in the birth rate, which had been stable for half a century. With the advent of such change and uncertainty, Isaac again found himself musing over his future.

Still a member of the Yeomanry, Scott witnessed Colonel Hassell attend his last training camp in 1871, having commanded the Westmorland and Cumberland Yeomanry for over forty years. Two years later, the annual training camp was held in Penrith, with 300 members of the Regiment descending on the town. The *Penrith Observer* reported on the show:

> *Visitors from far and wide have travelled to our market town to see the spectacle of the training exercises during the day, and listening to the Regimental Band as they give concerts during the evening. Business is also brisk for the publicans of the town as they provide accommodation for the yeomen and benefit from the visitors' custom.*

No doubt the ex-regular pointed his colleagues in the direction of his own pub and saw an atypical rise in his takings during that plentiful week.

Scott served a further four uneventful years with the part-timers before receiving his discharge in 1877. During this period, however, he found the promotion denied to most private soldiers in the regular army when he became Quartermaster (Sergeant-Major) Scott of the Edenhall Troop. (The purchase system in the regular army that continually disadvantaged the competent soldier and afforded promotion to his inefficient yet wealthy colleague was abolished in 1871.)

Many historians point to this period (1870s-1880s) as being the point at which the British Empire truly began its descent. Some contemporaries, who did not have the benefit of such retrospection, shared this view also: the poet of empire, Rudyard Kipling, who wrote memorable barrack room ballads about British soldiers, claimed for example that the British Empire would not last forever. Benjamin Disraeli, however, had had no such intimations as he had Victoria proclaimed Empress of India in 1877, twenty years before her Diamond Jubilee.

Isaac read in the *Penrith Herald* of the proclamation in January 1877. What would his thoughts have been? It had been twenty years since the outbreak of the Mutiny and race relations on the subcontinent remained brittle. Classic Disraelian spin however would have you believe that British India was still in its heyday. In truth, as in 1854 the British authorities were worrying more about the threat from Russian

Quartermaster Isaac Scott of the Westmorland and Cumberland Yeomanry

expansion than from internal challenges in India.

Was the government paying too much attention to its foreign dominions and neglecting its charitable obligations to its depressed homeland? That may have been the question on the lips of farmers throughout Britain but the truth was that the farmers in Cumberland never did suffer in the same way during the 1870s. In fact they actually benefited from the expansion of the railways to the county, and the depression suffered elsewhere, and so feared by locals, never actually took hold. When the Royal Show was held in the county in 1880, a report connected to the Farm Prize Competition praised the entrepreneurial skills of the local farmers:

> *There is no district in England so little affected by the agricultural depression as Cumberland and Westmorland... The farmers avoid ruin by unceasing work. All farms are crowded with Shorthorn cattle; good pure blood even on small farms and where no pedigree bull is available certified bulls are used. There is a general neglect of book-keeping but the Cumberland and Westmorland farmers are educated and hard-headed men... Whilst in the South, ruin has been gradually creeping upon the farming interest, in Cumberland and Westmorland there were few signs of any such calamity*

Whatever the reality, Isaac Scott had decided to take matters into his own hands three years earlier; like all good risk-takers, Scott believed in making his own luck. Shortly after leaving the Yeomanry, he sold the Grate and moved his young family to Carlisle.

✳ ✳ 9 ✳ ✳

Still an increasing conurbation during the final third of the nineteenth century, the Border City's population was in excess of 30,000 by the time the Scotts arrived. Isaac bought a house on Hope Street and found himself to be relatively wealthy compared to his Carlisle contemporaries. Although wards such as Caldewgate, Shaddongate and Denton Holme had seen dramatic improvement since the first half of the 19th century, they remained impoverished, and many of their inhabitants, having witnessed the demise of the cotton industry, were now employed as labourers or railway workers.

The other growth area in Carlisle during the late Victorian period was the development of shops. Prior to such expansion the city's commerce relied heavily on street markets. Market days were on Wednesday and Saturday. At harvest time, from 26th August, there was a continuous market known as the Great Fair, which lasted for 15 days. And whereas in theory anyone could set up a stall in any street, in practice, the 19th century turf warfare saw established stall-holders working their designated streets, with Caldewgate, still considered the Irish quarter of the city, known as 'Paddy's Market'. A sign of the changing times came in 1889 when the covered market was opened and outdoor traders came in off the streets.

By this time shopping indoors was quite the thing. The Industrial Revolution was good to many and now that they had wages to spend, the demand for mass-produced goods increased. Entrepreneurial flair is no new thing, as opportunism flourished in 1890s Carlisle: owners would convert their houses into shops and insert a large front window to catch the eye of the passing bargain hunter; and those who were really prepared to speculate to accumulate formed co-operative societies. The history of the Co-op, inspired as it was by the provision of self-managed mutual improvement societies, dated back to 1846. Fifteen years later the Carlisle South End Cooperative Society, consisting of several small stores dotted around the city, commenced business. Under the management of Creighton Pollock a decision was taken in February 1872 to expand the services offered to include tailoring and dressmaking.

It was with one of these co-operative societies that Isaac Scott found employment, not as a tailor (not at this stage, at least) but as a grocer. It wasn't long however before Scott was characteristically on the lookout for something else. He found it when his cyclical life saw him revert to his original trade. Although the rag trade had suffered considerably, there was

Isaac Scott's campaign medals

always room for a skilled tailor and Scott took up a position with Mr Robert Gibson, who ran his own shop in Bank Street. In so doing, he began an association with Gibson that was to last almost twenty years and was to result in his becoming a well known figure around the castle and in local military circles; for Gibson, as well as serving the ordinary customers of the city, acted as the Regimental Tailor to the Border Regiment.

In 1898 Isaac's second son, Charles (Charlie), met and began to court a young woollen machinist some four his years his junior called Bridget Thompson. Bridget was the daughter of boilersmith, Robert Thompson, whose own father was one of the thousands of Irish who migrated to Carlisle earlier in the century. The Thompsons were Roman Catholic and given that both Isaac and Jane were Anglican this caused some unrest in the Scott household, thought to be fuelled mainly by Jane's objections to the match. Family legend has it that Jane had become an old battle-axe of ocean-going proportions, who disliked and mistrusted Catholics intensely. That did not deter Charlie, however, and he married Bridget on 22nd February

1902. The two went on to produce five children of their own, the only grandchildren Isaac and Jane were to see.

Their first-born was Sydney, the apple of his parents' and grandparents' eyes. Jane would dote on the boy, who was christened in the Anglican Church and raised as a Protestant. Bridget had other ideas when it came to the four girls that followed young Sydney. Her four daughters were all christened and raised as Roman Catholics. One family anecdote recounts Jane never allowing Bridget into her home during the thirty years between her son's marriage and her own death. If this is true, Bridget had the last laugh, as all subsequent generations of the family were raised as Catholics!

The century that had seen so much innovation drew to a close and Britain once more rose to a patriotic frenzy and sent a task force to South Africa for its final Victorian military campaign. Like most old soldiers, Isaac was content to read about the exploits of his successors in the local press (both his former regiments served in the Boer War). And as the country stared uncertainly into the new century, the lady who gave her name to the period passed the crown to her son. *The Times* tried to capture the essence of Victoria in reporting her death in January 1901:

> *The Queen is dead. No language can express the sense of personal loss... Few of us, perhaps, have realized till now how large a part she had in the life of every one of us; how the thread of her life, in binding and strengthening like a golden weft, the warp of the nation's progress, has touched and brightened the life of each and all of her subjects.*

There can be no easy summary of the events and processes of Victoria's long reign, but outstanding achievements that benefited her subjects included the Education Act of 1870 that increased formal schooling to the nation's children by sevenfold; further parliamentary reform that ended up entitling the majority of the population to vote, from a niggardly three per cent at her accession (how ironic today, that when there is one hundred per cent entitlement, only thirty per cent turn out at elections); and the dire poverty experienced in the first half of the nineteenth century had at least been greatly reduced if not completely eradicated. On the downside, the British Army, on every continent of the globe, waged a staggering figure of over sixty major military campaigns as her empire sought expansion.

One of her subjects, a veteran of two of those campaigns, meanwhile, had taken up what was to be his final job. Isaac's friend and employer, Mr Gibson, had passed away in 1895 and with no natural heir and his premier tailor now a sexagenarian, his business ceased. (John Watt secured the lease on the premises after Gibson's death and his coffee shop remains in the

Syd Scott, Isaac's first grandchild

same location today.) The manager of one of the Co-operative stores on Botchergate, however, recognised there is no substitute for experience and was more than happy to employ the old soldier.

By the turn of the boom-and-bust century, wages were stagnating amongst the working populus, while prices continued to rise throughout the country. The Co-op therefore, was one of the most accessible stores for Carlisle's inhabitants. In 1904 the several small stores along Botchergate were consolidated into one. Several of the satellite stores continued to trade elsewhere but the new store became the central office and remained there for over ninety years.

The description of the store's ornate interior upon its opening read more like one of the great Edwardian liners that graced the high seas at the time. The Tailoring Department was entered on the ground floor where ready-made garments and hosiery could be purchased. The first floor directly above housed the woollen cutters and fitting rooms with the second floor used for storage. Isaac was employed in the new store as the senior tailor, and he and his colleagues worked on the third floor in the tailors' workroom; there was then a separate adjoining room for the numerous machinists. One of Isaac's apprentices, over eighty himself when interviewed, remembered his boss and the working environment with great affection.

Isaac and Jane were now living at 22 Finkle Street, opposite the castle. Although their second son, Charlie, had married and moved back into Caldewgate with his wife, Bridget, the four other grown-up children remained, for the time being, at least, with their parents, and it was at this time that the eldest son, Frank, reached the heights of his athletics career. Frank had gradually built a reputation as a fine athlete in the final decade of the 19th century, and during the first decade of the 20th was considered to be one of the best athletes in the county.

His name first appeared in a programme of an evening meeting of the Carlisle Amateur Cycling and Athletic Association, held at the Edenside cricket ground on 14th June 1894. He appeared at the meeting as a sprinter, coming in third in the final of the quarter mile open handicap. But then he discovered his forte was in the walking events, a popular feature of the many local sports meetings which were held around the county in those days and which drew a regular large following.

Amongst his early successes, Scott won 18 prizes: 14 firsts, three seconds and one third. In 23 major races during his career, his tally was 17 wins, three seconds and one third. In only two of these races did he not finish in the first three. One of these failures caused quite a stir among the local press

Finkle Street, Carlisle, c1905 (Ashley Kendall)

in 1903, when he competed in a race from Carlisle to Penrith. Leading the race by half a mile, Frank broke down exhausted just before the finish. When asked by the eager reporter, as to how he revived himself after such exhaustion, Frank replied, 'I drink brandy.'

Obviously a man of few words, Scott was soon back on fine form, letting his feet do the talking at the annual (and tongue-twisting) Lazonby Floral and Horticultural Society Show and Sports Programme. The newspaper report of the event conjures up images of Mr. Chumley-Warner doing a piece for Pathé News:

> *The three-mile walking race created much interest amongst the spectators. From the first it was seen that Scott, the man who broke down so near the finish of the Carlisle to Penrith walk, would win easily. As a matter of fact he lapped Carrick (Carlisle) twice and Nicol once. He finished in a very good time of 27 minutes 41 seconds. Nichol was second and Carrick was third. A fine effort by all concerned.*

Isaac would regularly be seen supporting his son and rubbing shoulders with the likes of the local MP, Claude Lowther, and the mayors of the day who would be there to present the prizes.

Even in those days, and at such a local level, athletics were not without their controversies. Frank himself commented on two disqualifications in his diary of 1904. He wrote:

> I won at Broughton sports again in 1904 in the three miles scratch race but when I finished they said I did not walk fair. I won at Whitehaven sports, in the one mile handicap but was disqualified for competing at unregistered meetings.

An indication of the popularity of race walking came in 1906, when it was introduced as an Olympic sport at the interim Athens Games. Races of 1500 metres and 3,000 metres, roughly the distances Frank and his competitors were racing locally, were held. In 1908 at the London Games these two walks were replaced with a 3500 metre walk as well as a 10-mile walk.

Both Frank and his father progressively became well known figures in the city, as press reports of his achievements usually commenced, 'Frank Scott, son of Crimean Veteran, Isaac Scott...'

As for Isaac himself, his final military hurrah came in November 1907 with the arrival of a letter from the Mayor, who had in turn been contacted by the *Daily Telegraph* newspaper. Throughout 1907 the newspaper had printed recollections of the Indian Mutiny and this culminated in the proprietors, in conjunction with the War Office and the Admiralty, organizing a Christmas dinner to be held for all surviving veterans to commemorate the fiftieth anniversary. The dinner itself was to be held on 23rd December at the Royal Albert Hall in London.

Scott and two other veterans from Carlisle (Messrs Dunnett and Brooks of the 5th Fusiliers and the 34th Regiment respectively) travelled to the capital the day before the celebrations were to be held. Over 2,000 veterans were greeted upon their arrival, and the old soldiers were taken by motorbus for a tour of the sights of the city prior to their transfer to their various hotels.

The weather of the 23rd was miserable. The incessant drizzle from the low grey skies, however, did not put off thousands of spectators who gathered outside the hall to witness the arrival of the veterans. They themselves gathered in Kensington Gardens, where they were inspected by the guest of honour, Lord Roberts, a veteran of the campaign himself as a junior lieutenant. The men were then allowed to meet up with former comrades prior to entering the hall. Among the former colleagues Isaac met and no doubt exchanged stories with that afternoon was the retired CaptainHenry Marshall who, as a young Cornet, was Private Scott's first commanding officer as he set out on his Crimean odyssey in 1855.

Isaac's son, champion walker Frank Scott

111

The medal-laden, leathery old veterans certainly impressed the *Telegraph's* reporter, who wrote the following day:

> It was quite striking to behold and worth coming a long way to see the manner in which old warriors, widely separated by rank and class, met each other as friends in the comradeship of service against the enemy.

The venue was decorated with coloured flags and banners: British red, white and blue and Indian light blue and gold, and as the old soldiers entered they were presented with a briar pipe that sported a silver ring with the dates 1857-1907 on it. They also received two ounces of tobacco, a box of snuff and a book published by the *Daily Telegraph* containing their own reports and reminiscences of the campaign that had been printed in the newspaper throughout the year.

Distinguished guests included the erstwhile champion in verse of the British soldier, Rudyard Kipling, who wrote a special poem for the occasion simply entitled *1857-1907*. During the dinner the band of the Royal Artillery entertained the guests; cheers and applause from the floor constantly interrupted Lord Roberts' speech as he made reference to certain names, places and actions; telegrams were read out from absentees such as the Viceroy of India, Lord Minto, Lord Kitchener who had succeeded Roberts in South Africa during the Boer War, Sir Evelyn Wood VC (Isaac's colleague from Baroda) who was too ill to attend the dinner, and even the King himself. Two other noteworthy absentees were William Howard Russell of *The Times*, who had reported with such distinction but who had died in 1907; and Jacob Reed. Although Jacob and Isaac served in the same campaigns, the former was considerably older. In relation to your author, there was actually a generation between them. As we learned earlier, Jacob died thirty years earlier.

The splendid occasion concluded with the reciting of Kipling's poem, the singing of Auld Lang Syne and the National Anthem and the sounding of The Last Post, in honour of the men and women who died in the atrocities. The old warriors were then returned to their hotels, before returning home on Christmas Eve.

In July of the following year the recently formed Carlisle Veteran Relief Fund granted Isaac 2s per week. Alas, he was not to enjoy this luxury for too long as in late August of the same year he suffered a burst blood vessel in his leg and was rushed into hospital to be operated on. Although he received prompt medical attention, the staff at the Cumberland Infirmary could not prevent a blood infection taking hold; and he was allowed to return home to spend his last few days.

Isaac Scott

William Pearson (Penrith Museum)

Some of the most eminent Victorians lived to great ages: Robert Browning and Charles Darwin lived into their seventies while Alfred Lord Tennyson and John Ruskin both topped eighty before their innings came to an end. It is a misconception, however, to think that large numbers of Victorian men became aged greybeards like Penrithians Isaac Scott and William Pearson. Life expectancy for middle-aged men had improved in the 1890s but it was the exception rather than the rule for men to live into their seventies and eighties — grandfathers were pretty thin on the ground until well into the twentieth century.

Isaac was one of the exceptions, but on Wednesday 30th September 1908 he died of peritonitis at his home on Finkle Street: he was 74. Recognition of Scott and his achievements had gradually increased during his thirty years in Carlisle and he was of course a well known character in local military circles, being acknowledged not only for his work as a tailor for the officers of The Border Regiment in the castle, but for his own campaigns of the mid-nineteenth century. It is appropriate then that the military theme that ran throughout his life was continued and concluded on the day of his burial. He was honoured by receiving a military funeral on Friday 2nd October.

At noon his body was transferred from his home to the castle. From there Isaac's coffin, draped with the Union Flag, left the castle at 2pm and proceeded along the people-lined Castle Street on its way to Carlisle Cemetery.

There was a firing party furnished by men of the Depot of The Border Regiment, and non commissioned officers of the local regiment and Westmorland & Cumberland Yeomanry acted as pall-bearers. Captain Morton with thirty NCOs and men also attended, along with numerous representatives from the local Territorial Forces.

Distinguished mourners included the Mayor and Mayoress and Major Legard of his former regiment who brought a splendid wreath of white blooms, which bore the inscription: 'With deepest sympathy from all ranks of the 17th (Duke of Cambridge's Own) Lancers.' Also in attendance were two of the Mutiny veterans who had accompanied Isaac to London the previous year to commemorate the 50th anniversary, Messrs Dunnett and Brooks. The (unrelated) military chaplain, Reverend H E Scott, read the burial service. At the conclusion of the service, three volleys were fired over the grave and the buglers of the 3rd Border Regiment sounded The Last Post.

It is interesting to note that when his headstone was erected it bore the inscription 'Crimean Veteran'. Whereas this is perfectly true, Scott saw little or no action during this glorious campaign. Yet his heroics, along with many

Isaac Scott's funeral (Jim Templeton)

of his colleagues who distinguished themselves during the rather less celebrated (and perhaps more shameful) Indian Mutiny campaign went virtually unreported.

As for the local veteran's passing, the press paid tribute by giving full details of his various exploits in his obituary. The *Carlisle Journal* actually described him as 'the only man born on Cumberland soil to take part in the Crimea and Mutiny campaigns'. A tribute certainly, but cruelly inaccurate; cruel that is on the local men of the local 34th (Cumberland) and 55th (Westmorland) Regiments who served during the period, as well as Isaac's fellow Penrithian and near neighbour, Trooper William Pearson of the 4th Light Dragoons, who survived the Charge of the Light Brigade.

POSTSCRIPT

Another Cumbrian with Crimean and Mutiny connections who deserves mention is, of course, our own Jacob Reed. It is interesting to compare the lives (and deaths) of Reed and Scott. The former was a pauper who felt he had to join the army; the latter, from a relatively comfortable background, chose to join. The circles Jacob moved in were also very different from those of Isaac. Reed left the army and lived out his life in quiet anonymity. Isaac did not court celebrity but found it anyway due to

Isaac Scott's headstone in Carlisle Cemetery

his presence around the castle and his casual schmoozing with local dignitaries (through his own achievements, and those of his son Frank). Although their military service and achievements are remarkably similar, their respective deaths could not be more different. Jacob died: we don't know how, we don't know exactly when, and we don't even know where he was laid to rest. When Isaac passed away, the city came out in all its pomp and circumstance to mourn the death of one of its finest. Perhaps if Jacob's headstone is ever found, it's my guess that his epitaph will simply read: 'It's not what you know but who you know!'

A few days after Isaac's death on 10th October, his daughter, Amy, purchased five plots around his grave, although only four of these plots were eventually used, by his widow, Jane, daughter, Amy, eldest son, Frank and Frank's wife, Mary.

The endless conflicts witnessed and experienced by Victorians such as Isaac did nothing to secure world peace, or even the imperial peace for which he fought. In the very week that he died, the *Mid Cumberland & North Westmorland Herald* reported on 'The Eastern Crisis', the tearing up of the Treaty of Berlin, the proclamation of independence for Bulgaria, and the annexing of Bosnia Herzegovina by the Austro-Hungarian Empire. A six-year-long fuse burned before this tinderbox exploded in 1914.

Isaac's youngest son, also Isaac but known by his second name of Nelson, took part in the First World War, serving in the Labour Corps. He was the only one of Isaac's three sons to serve in the military. Isaac's widow, Jane, moved to Edward Street in Carlisle to live with her son, Frank, until her death in 1935. Frank resumed his athletics career after the war, winning high profile races up to and including 1920.

When the childless Frank died, his estate, which included two houses, sold for £900 passed to his younger brother. Charlie was a man of his generation: hard worker, hard smoker, even harder drinker. It was this last pursuit of Charlie's that accounted for most of the Scott dynasty's wealth.

DAN DALEY

Joiner & Private with the Volunteer Battalion of the Border Regiment

✳ ✳ 1 ✳ ✳

The final character to take centre stage in this volume is one with whom I share a surname. Ironically, unlike Jacob Reed and Isaac Scott, Dan Daley is not a direct relative of mine: he is a collateral ancestor. Both he and I are descended from the Daley clan who sent three of their sons over from Ireland in the early years of the 19th century. The sons in question were brothers: Henry, John and Patrick; like so many of their countrymen, the three came to Carlisle, chasing the dream of health and good living in the cotton-rich city. But the dream was an illusion and like the thousands of other Irish immigrants, the three ended up scratching round to make ends meet.

As the Carlisle natives were getting restless in 1820, Patrick decided to escape the claustrophobic, urban death trap and move south to Penrith. While his two brothers remained (labouring and weaving) in the Border City, Patrick moved into the agricultural industry in the burgeoning Penrith area. In 1824, he married a fellow Catholic migrant from Tyrone and a year later, their first child was born, a daughter named Ann, after her mother, and their son Daniel followed in 1832.

As we saw earlier, William Scott (Isaac's father) was a tenant farmer around this period, making money from the land, while keeping the land owner sweet with his rent. Patrick Daley came further down the agricultural pecking order, working as a farm labourer. By adulthood, his son, Daniel, was following in his father's footsteps by joining a profession that accounted for 21 per cent of the working population of Britain in 1851. In the same year it was identified that 80 per cent of farms in England and Wales were 'small farms' — comprised of 100 or fewer acres — and this was certainly representative in Cumberland where large farms and cottagers' smallholdings formed only a small fragment of the industry.

Although father and son shared the same profession, the two were quite distinct from one another. Patrick Daley, the married waged labourer, was literally employed on a week-to-week basis, receiving a wage of 11s 6d. His son, Daniel, by contrast, was a farm servant and was paid less (around 7s), but he benefited over his father in that he was hired on an annual or half-yearly contract. These contracts were obtained at the hiring fairs, which took place all over the county at either Whitsuntide (week commencing with Whit Sunday, the seventh Sunday after Easter) or the biggest fairs at Martinmas in November. These fairs grew in importance during the Agrarian Revolution when demand for more farm labourers reached fever pitch.

On the appointed day, Daniel would present himself at the Penrith hiring fair to earn himself a contract. He would be one of hundreds who poured into the town: farm servants of both sexes, arriving on foot; farmers, there to do the hiring, with their carts; and scores of onlookers, packed in till the marketplace was filled with moving crowds from end to end. Business was mixed with pleasure as merry-go-rounds and stalls dotted the streets, while the constant sounds of buying and selling, bartering and hiring echoed around the town.

The actual hiring itself was a sort of 19th century speed dating. Farmers were there to hire their servants for the forthcoming year. Before doing so they would take a good look round, and when they saw a young man or lad who appeared, from his build and healthy look, likely to suit their purpose, the master would accost him, and, after asking a few questions as to the other's capabilities — his former place, and so forth — they came to the important question of wage. If both parties were agreed — and to be honest, the servant didn't have much bargaining power — the deal was done; x marked the spot on the contract as far as the illiterate servant was concerned, and the farmer would give his new hand half a crown or so to welcome him on board. The labourer would then disappear into the nearest 'hedge' alehouse or beer shop (converted cottages, as distinct from the principal town inns frequented by farmers and skilled craftsmen) and celebrate by pouring the said half a crown's worth of heady home brew down his neck. Ritual complete, his six-monthly or yearly contract would then begin.

Such was the system that turned the agricultural wheels in the mid 19th century. If this seems like an uncertain, hand-to-mouth existence, it was, but then both the weekly wage earners, and those on longer contracts in arable Cumberland were paid significantly more — almost twice as much in fact — than their counterparts elsewhere in the country.

Once in employment, Daniel's working year was a tough one. Throughout the seasons the farm labourer would work long hours, depending on the light and weather conditions, and have little time for leisure activities. The only noteworthy events to break up the yearly cycle for the farm hands were the minor festivities laid on by their employers at

Penrith town centre in the late 19th century (John Hurst)

key times of the year, such as harvest time. Working his employee hard throughout the year, the farmer recognised the importance of such occasions and his family would enter wholeheartedly into the festivities with his farm labourers, which contributed in no small degree to foster a good feeling between masters and men. The only real holiday worthy of the name which the farm servants enjoyed in the course of the year was Martinmas week itself, the quietest time of the year on the farms. During this week labourers would attend another hiring fair and their working year would commence again.

In 1862 Daniel married Jane Sanderson, a local girl with an upbringing equally as tough as as her new husband's, ever since her birth in the Penrith Workhouse in 1837. Other than his modest salary, the only support Daniel received was from the Foresters. They were a Friendly Society that, because of the insecurities of urban or rural employment, offered a kind of protection and service to its members; they were part co-operative, part union, part insurance company. Friendly Societies had been around in small numbers since the end of the 18th century but it was in the first half of the 19th that they really took off, and Cumberland and Westmorland were not slow in following the expansionist lead displayed by their northern neighbours Lancashire, Yorkshire and Derbyshire. Members made regular financial contributions in return for the society's assistance in relieving the sick and distressed, and providing a decent burial for the dead.

Often the Friendly Societies became focal points for community life and this was certainly true in Penrith: monthly meetings were held and the 'sociability' aspect was an important feature with societies organising

121

concerts, dances and processions to raise funds for the benefit of their members. By the time Daniel married Jane in 1862, The Foresters, The Oddfellows and The Druids were all well established Friendly Societies in Penrith. Although never strictly intended to be affiliated to religious denominations, The Foresters was mainly a Catholic organisation and, therefore, smaller than its two cousins. The Oddfellows had originally modelled their society on some of the principles and practices of Freemasonry. They gradually developed their own rites, ceremonies, robes and regalia, together with closely guarded and secret activities within the Lodges. The three societies would also hold joint events and annual galas.

Daniel and Jane celebrated the birth of their first child, Joseph, a year after their wedding. As the first ten years of their marriage progressed, emotional and physical hardship came increasingly to the fore. As the great depression in the agricultural industry began to take hold, so prices dropped, farms closed and the agricultural labour market degenerated into a countrywide survival of the fittest challenge. And this, despite Cumberland not being as badly affected as counties elsewhere, is where Daniel Daley started to struggle. He was a chronic asthmatic, and faced with competition from younger, fitter men, he was a less attractive prospect to the choosy employers at the hiring fairs. When work in the fields ran out completely, the only expedient open to Daniel was to take any work available in and around the Penrith area: labourer, builder, railway navvy.

Casual work may have come and gone but the production line of little Daleys continued throughout the decade: Isabella (1871), Alfred (1873) and Mary Jane (1876) joined their older brother, Joseph, and parents and Daniel's niece, Ann, and her daughter, Caroline; all crammed into a tiny two bed-roomed house in the middle of the town.

The newspapers that kept Penrithians abreast of local and world events were the *Penrith Herald* and the *Penrith Observer*. By the 1870s they were not only reporting on the Agricultural Depression at home, but were focusing their attentions on world events, and in particular on the European Empires' machinations in Africa. To the forefront in these machinations was, of course, Britain, and what were snippets of current events in 1870 would develop over the next thirty years, leading to a chapter of grand history by the century's end; and this piece of history would not just snake its way back to Britain but directly to the door of the Daley household in sleepy little Penrith.

How Britain came to be in Africa in the first place is an all too familiar tale of pocket-lining empire builders who did not know when to stop. As with India, the European Empires had had their collective eye on the Dark

Continent for some time, and by the final quarter of the 19th century they became embroiled in what became known as the Scramble for Africa. Perhaps the carve-up of Africa would be a better term for what went on in that final quarter of the 19th century, as imperialistic Europeans bought, sold, bartered and stole from each other and locals alike, to claim ownership of the 10,000 independent African kingdoms. By the turn of the century, the 10,000 kingdoms had been turned into 40 European colonies (with Britain owning half of them), and the Scramble for Africa was drawing to a close. There was only one African tribe left who refused to bow to the might of the British Empire, but they were white, not black.

The Boers (the word means farmer) were descended from a mixture of Dutch, French and German settlers. Generally a quiet people, the Boers were fiercely Calvinist and contemptuous of blacks and foreign settlers alike; they sought to preserve their austere farming communities without their European masters interfering in their dealings. They lived in the four colonies that made up 19th century South Africa: Cape Colony, Natal, the Transvaal and the Orange Free State. After decades of prickly relations between the British and the Boers, 1852 saw the wretchedly poor countries of the Transvaal and Orange Free State, both perceived by the British to be of no value or importance, granted their independence. This 'everyone's-a-winner' approach seemed to solve the problem of the troublesome Boers: Britain had two colonies, and the Boers had two colonies. That was until 1870 when vast quantities of diamond ore were discovered in and around the Orange Free State town of Kimberly. The town was promptly annexed into the [British] Cape Colony.

Just as the Scramble for Africa was getting under way, about five and a half thousand miles due north in Penrith Cumberland, Daniel Daley was born on 12th January 1878. Dan was the fifth child of Daniel and Jane Daley. He was joining a family packed like sardines into a tiny house on Redfurns Yard, one of several tiny yards that dotted the length of Rowcliffe Lane, one of the oldest areas of the town. Although only eight feet wide at its narrowest point, the lane, when it was called Post Office Lane, was used as one of Penrith's main streets. By the latter half of the 19th century it was an impoverished area that was home to scores of working class families, and provided shelter for countless Irish navvies or wayfarers who were passing through the town.

The Daleys may well have been near neighbours of the Scotts (Isaac's family), who were living and working at the Grate Inn, a few hundred yards away, but they did not enjoy the relative wealth and stability of their pub-owning contemporaries. Instead, they relied on the benevolence offered by

Rowcliffe Lane, Penrith, in the late 19th century (Penrith Museum)

the Foresters Society and the uncertainty of the agricultural industry following the repeal of the Corn Laws.

As we have seen elsewhere, tragedy was a regular occurrence for the working classes of the day. Victorian families might have been bigger still, had it not been for a continuing high rate of infant mortality, which varied significantly from one part of the country, and from one occupation to another. Urban infant mortality was naturally worse (30 per cent higher than in rural areas) but there was no rhyme, reason nor pattern to such tragedy and the Daleys, in their overcrowded, unsanitary dwelling, were no exception to such indiscriminate loss. On 21st July 1878, barely six months after young Dan's birth, his infant cousin Caroline died in the family's squalid surroundings aged just eleven months.

✳ ✳ 2 ✳ ✳

The Daley children attended St Catherine's Catholic School on Drover's Lane, established in 1870 as a result of the Education Act. (An example of the growth in the Catholic population of Penrith is demonstrated by the demand for a church and school in the town. The first were built in 1850.) Young Dan's big day came on 10th January 1881, when his sister Mary and brother Alfie accompanied him on his first day to school. The three siblings left their home on a dark, bitterly cold winter's morning and picked their way down the icy cobbles of Rowcliffe Lane. The school log that day gives a fascinating picture of the austere environment experienced by teacher and pupil alike:

> School re-opened today after the Christmas holidays. Only a poor attendance this morning owing to the severity of the weather. Great improvement in the attendance this afternoon, although due to the hard frost, children in all the standards write on slates instead of copying books owing the ink being frozen.

The curriculum consisted of reading, handwriting, arithmetic, grammar, spelling, needlework (an insight into how the young females were prepared for adulthood and its domestic need for self sufficiency), and, last but by no means least, religious instruction, on which a great emphasis was placed, especially in preparation for the visits of Father Edward O'Dwyer, the parish priest. As the Catholic Church fully sponsored its schools in the 19th century, so the parish priest acted as the 'manager' of the school. This was the role of Father O'Dwyer, and it was he who wrote the annual end of year reports. So when Father O'Dwyer visited, you were on your best behaviour, and if you weren't, the cane was produced, as Dan's older brother, Alfie, found out to his cost in November 1884. The school log noted that: 'Alfred Daley was caned for disobedience and laziness.' Otherwise the children were well cared for with qualified teachers and teachers' helpers regularly escorting them on day trips to Cockermouth and the Lakes.

At the same time that three-year-old Dan Daley was starting school in January 1881, Britain was preparing for war again, this time in South Africa. The cause of the war stemmed back to 1877 when, under the pretext that there was anarchy in the Transvaal, Britain annexed the little Boer republic and declared it a crown colony two years later. The Boers hated the British rule (who didn't?) and the time-bomb relationship between the two ignited in 1881 when a dispute over taxes erupted into the first (but not the last) Boer War.

Despite coverage of the 'Transvaal War' in the press, it attracted little attention amongst the British public. If it was gaining little attention nationally, it was certainly acquiring virtually no attention locally. The editor of the *Penrith Observer* appealed to his readers on 15th March 1881:

> *Do the British public realise that the so-called independence of the Transvaal means nearly over a quarter of a million natives will be cast into what is practically slavery? These unfortunates are flogged and shot like dogs if they are sick or run away. Why are the Anti-Slavery and Aborigines Protection Society silent?*

The same edition carried the far more interesting and higher profile story on the assassination of the Tsar in Russia.

If his readership in general showed little enthusiasm for the story, the Daleys of Redfurns Yard paid no attention to it whatsoever. Their charity began and ended at home, as in March 1881 they were coming to terms with a tragic thunderbolt that had ripped through their home only two weeks earlier. The head of the household, the asthmatic 48-year-old Daniel Daley, succumbed to a bronchial infection on 28th February and his wife, Jane, was left to bring up her children alone.

With no time to play the Victoria-type grief-stricken widow (the queen disappeared from public view for a decade after the loss of her beloved Albert in 1861), Jane promptly set about providing for her family by taking a job as a laundress in a the nearby George Hotel and by taking in yet another relative, her brother, William Sanderson, as lodger and substitute father to her children.

The distant war in South Africa passed by virtually unnoticed in the provinces of Britain. Why should it be otherwise? It was a short conflict and was concluded with the signing of the Pretoria Convention on 3rd August 1881. But its significance would have far-reaching effects in terms of both time and distance. Britain hadn't put the military might behind the campaign and the net result was that she lost the war — the only one she was to lose throughout the 19th century. The treaty that followed gave Transvaalers 'complete self-government, subject to suzerainty of Her Majesty.' This was a bit of a halfway house in reality: Britain got off the hook by retaining control over external relations, retaining the right to move its troops throughout the country, and holding a veto over laws affecting the Bantu (the native tribespeople whom the Boers had no compunction about harassing and demeaning). The Transvaalers, content with their success in retaining their independence, also agreed to permit foreigners to enter, live

Rowcliffe Lane, Penrith, in the late 19th century (Penrith Museum)

and work in the country without interference and to exempt from military service the British subjects registered as British residents.

A messy business perhaps, but in Britain the apparently insignificant happenings in South Africa barely registered on the scale of importance. There was a certain feeling of capitulation and humiliation within the Westminster village of 1881, but this was overcome by the general feel-good-factor that came in a year when London, with a population of 4.5 million, was declared the largest city in the world.

If the Transvaal Boers thought they could finally settle down to a mind-their-own-business existence, their world was soon to be turned upside down. In 1887 a sixty-mile-long ridge called the Witwatersrand (the Rand for short), running east to west thirty miles south of Pretoria, was uncovered as the largest gold field in the world. The significance of the discovery was not lost on the Transvaal President, Paul Kruger, who announced, 'Instead of rejoicing we would do better to weep, for this gold will cause our country to be soaked in blood.'

Sure enough, within months foreigners (or *uitlanders* as the Boers called them) started flooding into South Africa. The (mainly British) uitlanders were soon outnumbering the Boers in the Transvaal and made no attempt to adopt the ways of the local population: they wanted things done their way.

In a tiny paragraph in the *Penrith Observer* in November 1887, the editor commented on the 'booming gold mines' of South Africa and how this was leading to development of the hitherto troublesome country. It is debatable whether his piece was even read, let alone understood, in Redfurns Yard. At number three, the head of the household was more interested in domestic life than international or even national politics.

Unlike her late husband, Jane Daley was a non-Catholic but her determination to raise her children as her husband intended is evidenced by her continuing to take the children to church and having them all confirmed between 1884 and 1888. She also witnessed her eldest son, Joseph, marry Margaret Watson in October 1884. (Dan jnr was confirmed with his sister, Mary Jane, on 22nd October 1888; he took his grandfather's name, Patrick). Jane herself made the personal step by converting to the Catholic Church when she was baptised on 16th April 1887, aged 50.

As a parent watches his or her brood grow, a hope is kindled that one day they will leave the family nest and set up on their own, leaving the exhausted parent to enjoy their newfound freedom, safe in the knowledge that their job is done. For Jane Daley the reality was very different: instead of diminishing, her already large family continued to burgeon as her son and daughter-in-law celebrated the birth of their first child in 1890. Interestingly, it was Jane herself who acted as godmother to John Alfred, her first grandchild. The joy occasioned by the birth was tempered by the fact that her son, his wife and their baby had to be somehow shoehorned into the already overcrowded home. In an effort to accommodate her family in a little more comfort, she managed to obtain a lease across town, where she could benefit from the relative luxury of a four-roomed dwelling on Stricklandgate.

Jane's youngest, Dan, completed his schooling in 1892; his elder sister Mary had completed hers two years earlier but had remained at St Catherine's, working as a teaching assistant (she would go on to utilise the needlework and sowing skills that were so prevalent at the time by taking up an apprenticeship as a dressmaker). For his part, the young man obtained a position of apprentice joiner with the Middlegate Brewery.

Although life continued to be hard for the Daley family during the last decade of the century, one significant advantage they enjoyed over previous generations was the increased leisure time available to all classes. As the 1880s progressed the majority of the working classes gained a six and a half day week. The Bank Holiday Act (1871) had provided statutory holidays and the need to fill all of this excessive leisure time saw society develop an increase in its recreational activities: brass bands, horticultural societies, choral and amateur dramatic societies appeared in almost every town, while football and cricket clubs flourished, as did the volunteers: the forerunners of the Territorial Army. (In his excellent *History of Penrith*, 1894, William Furness reported amusingly, although probably unintentionally: '... a new organisation, the Penrith Total Abstinence Society came into existence, with a great flourish of trumpets, but as yet it has made slow progress.')

As we saw earlier through the exploits of champion walker Frank Scott, athletics and cycling events attracted competitors of all ages from around the county. When it came to free time, it seems there was no end of choice for the modern-day teenager compared to his grandfather or even his father. And if you were a youngster in Penrith, there was no fear of missing out on this national trend for health and lifestyle either; while Frank was competing elsewhere, the town of his birth was already heavily sports-minded, with thriving Rugby Union, cricket, bowling, swimming and cycling clubs, even before Thomas Edwin Fletcher proposed forming an Association Football Club in 1894. The *Mid Cumberland and North Westmorland Herald* voiced its concerns in May of that year:

Professionalism in Association Football, has led to more robustness on the pitch and increased the catalogue of deaths and injuries...Nothing is to be more deprecated than the tendency to convert what should be a pleasant and healthy pastime into a brutalising and money-making business.

One of Fletcher's arguments had been that Penrith would benefit from an established team that could compete around the county and what's more, with the addition of a dedicated playing area, it would reduce the likelihood of anti-social behaviour, or as it was put delicately at the time, it would help to 'keep young men out of mischief'. Fletcher's vision became a reality when the Local Board of Health released the land known as Kilgour's Field (now Southend Road) and his club was formed on 27th September 1894.

Young men flocked to the club, among them 16-year-old Dan Daley, who quickly impressed the club's officials. A contemporary report illustrates how clichéd football reporting has changed little in one hundred years when young Daley was described as 'a tricky forward with an eye for goal'. The new form of football also caught the imagination of the townsfolk, with four-figure crowds reported within two years of the club's formation. In 1899 the establishment of football in the town was confirmed when the Penrith and District Football League was formed. The six founder clubs were Working Men (later Penrith F.C.), Penrith United, Blencathra Rovers, Threlkeld, Carleton Rovers and Patterdale.

The warm feeling and community spirit had never been so good in Penrith, and it was just about to get better as they prepared to pay homage to the woman who dominated this man's world.

✳ ✳ 3 ✳ ✳

'**G**reat empires seldom last long...the wrong choice for England will reduce her to the level of Spain.' The Cambridge historian, John Sealy, wrote these visionary words. Sealy was not the only powerful voice prophesying doom for the British Empire: that champion-in-verse of the British soldier, Rudyard Kipling, had been expressing his concerns for years. But no one paid much attention to these killjoys as Queen Victoria's Diamond Jubilee approached in 1897. Her empire now stretched over a fifth of the planet, the biggest in the world's history. As one quarter of the world's population saluted the union flag every night, so 22nd June 1897 was to be the biggest global party ever known. As springtime arrived, preparations in the imperial capitals of London, Delhi, Cape Town and Sydney were all well under way: parades and bands, parties and banners were to be the order of the day. Towns and cities throughout the empire were following their lead, as all classes prepared for the big day, which was to be bigger and better than the Queen's Golden Jubilee ten years earlier.

In Penrith, a committee was established in March to make arrangements for the town's celebrations. Although preparations were hampered by a measles epidemic (something that saw the schools close for a fortnight in May to stop the disease spreading), by midsummer's day everything was in place. There was to be a parade through the streets, events for children and the elderly alike, and a firework display on Beacon Pike, overlooking the town.

The townsfolk rose to bright sunshine on the morning of 22nd June 1897, and by ten o'clock those participating in the parade had assembled, appropriately enough, on Victoria Road. Half an hour later, the mounted Superintendent of Police led off, followed by the cavalry band and horse parade, the marching Penrith Volunteers, the urban councillors, Fire Brigade, and Post Office staff. Bringing up the rear of the parade were the three Friendly Societies: The Foresters, The Druids and The Oddfellows and their band. Among their number was Dan Daley, the young joiner who had carried on his father's and his grandfather's example by joining the Foresters Society.

On they marched, through streets bedecked with banners and union flags, while cheering and anthem-singing crowds waved and danced their approval. The parade wound its way down Stricklandgate, in front of the Daley house, with Jane and her family cheering her youngest son as he

Queen Victoria's Diamond Jubilee celebrations (Frank Boyd)

marched past. As it passed the houses from which the townsfolk watched, the householders joined on to the rear of the train as it marched towards the town centre—a procession that took ninety minutes.

As midday approached, the crowd surged forward in Market Square to get a better view of the dignitaries on the balcony of the George Hotel. Mounted Yeomanry struggled to marshal the enthusiastic crowd but as the clock struck twelve, the bands struck up and the whole town stood to attention and sang the national anthem. At that moment, as the powerful and moving strains of *God Save the Queen* echoed through the small lanes and streets of Penrith, Victoria herself was attending a thanksgiving service at St Paul's in London. 50,000 troops from across the globe had been despatched to London to lead a parade for their monarch who sat, safe in the knowledge that a quarter of the world's population were paying her homage. The parade in London stretched for six miles and was accompanied by Edward Elgar's *Imperial March*, composed especially for the Jubilee.

The day was far from over in Penrith, as Dan and his colleagues from the Friendly Societies held a gala on Foundry Field for the town's senior citizens (literally, Victoria's contemporaries). By mid afternoon it was the children's turn to form a procession and sing for their Jubilee treat of a medal in the form of a Maltese Cross, two buns and an orange (these were the days before your Jubilee coins and mugs). Bands played in the town centre through the midsummer evening before the day's festivities were brought to a close with the illumination of Beacon Pike and the firework display. Dan and his family returned to their tiny cottage in their small Cumberland town in jovial mood, a wonderful day having been had by all. 'Penrith did Her Majesty proud,' exclaimed the *Observer* the following day. The following year, Penrithians showed further loyalty to the queen when they built Jubilee Cottage Hospital on Beacon Edge.

For the swollen-headed imperialists in Whitehall and Fleet Street, it didn't get any better than this. But elsewhere in Victoria's empire, things were not all sweetness and light. In South Africa the stubborn Boers had fought and defeated the British twenty years earlier to retain their independence; now, with the sympathy and backing of Germany, they were not about to relinquish their sovereignty over the two remaining independent republics, the Transvaal and the Orange Free State. This obstinacy did not deter the new High Commissioner to South Africa, Sir Alfred Milner, as he travelled to the Cape with greater zeal than ever to wrestle the Transvaal with all its riches away from the Boers.

For twenty years, British gold-hungry imperialists had attempted to take control of the independent state by fair means or foul; this included planning an attempted coup d'état in 1895. The Jameson Raid, named after the man who dreamt it up, failed and the British Government pleaded their innocence to the watching world, claiming there was no official involvement in the plot. Now, two years later, Milner was determined to see the Transvaal annexed, preferably through diplomacy, but if military action was called for he was not averse to that either. The pretext under which Milner intended to pressure the Transvaal was the old question of allowing the uitlanders the vote. This was not without irony, as many foreigners didn't necessarily want the vote; they were more interested in stripping the Republic of its assets and making off back to Blighty with the swag.

As the High Commissioner in South Africa put as much pressure on as he could, his boss in London, Joseph Chamberlain (Minister for the Colonies), with the eyes of the world on him found himself dithering, not knowing what to do for the best. It was clear Milner was itching for reform in the Transvaal but Chamberlain remained unconvinced about war at this

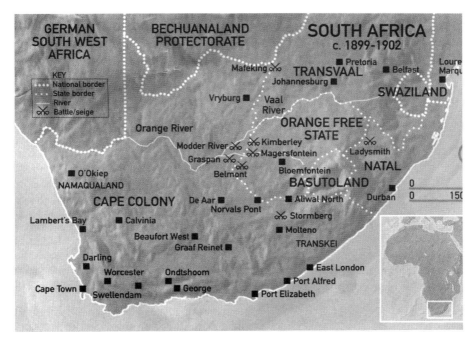

South Africa in 1899

point and told the House:

> A war in South Africa would be one of the most serious wars that
> could possibly be waged. It would be in the nature of a civil war. It
> would be a long war, and a costly war, and, as I have pointed out
> already, it would leave behind embers of strife which I believe
> generations would be hardly long enough to extinguish.

He was absolutely right of course, and would be proved so, but the wily
Milner knew exactly which buttons to press within the corridors of power
both at home and abroad, and after two years of chivvying through intense
letter writing and sexing up the odd dossier here and there, Milner was able
to persuade Chamberlain to change his opinion. What he was angling for
was both ingenious and sinister: the thousands of Britons who had poured
into the Transvaal looking for gold, and who now outnumbered Boers of
voting age throughout the entire country, would vote out President Kruger
and thereby win the country for Britain without the need for war. It was an
empire-building scheme that would make any Bond villain proud. Where
Milner let himself down was in his underestimating the Boers and his own

lack of military knowledge.

The British press seemed ambivalent to the machinations at this point. Rumblings of trouble filled column inches in the broadsheets, but by the time they filtered down into the provinces there was no indication of the disastrous series of events that would lead many local men abroad. The *Mid Cumberland and North Westmorland Herald* reported in April 1899:

> *Reports from South Africa suggest that further problems lie ahead regarding the question of sovereignty over the independent state of the Transvaal. It was this little country that caused so much trouble almost twenty years ago that eventually led to war. The seemingly endless question over the right to vote appears to be causing the latest dispute.*

In the Transvaal itself, President Paul Kruger remained reluctant to permit the uitlanders any form of political power and continued to deny the British demands for franchise. Across the border in the Orange Free State, meanwhile, its President, Marthinus Steyn, realised that the head-in-the-sand approach would not work with the meddlesome British. Although there were no uitlanders in his Republic (mind you, there was no gold either), Steyn recognised the danger for all concerned if war broke out. He therefore offered to host a conference with Kruger and Milner in his capital, Bloemfontein, in the first week of June 1899. During the conference, Kruger offered Milner several concessions outside of Britain's claim to rule the Transvaal, but his conciliatory offers fell on deaf ears and Milner walked out of the conference to set about adopting Plan B instead: march an army from the Cape Colony north east through the Orange Free State and take the Transvaal by force. Once President Steyn realised Milner was hell bent on military action, he was quick to side with his cross-border Boer cousins: Milner had only succeeded in doubling his problems.

He returned to Cape Colony and set about transforming the 12,000 British troops, then in southern Africa, into an army of 50,000 men. As he ordered his troops to move towards the borders of the two Republics, reinforcements were sent out from Britain in September 1899, and Kruger and Steyn acknowledged that Britain intended to destroy the independence of their countries by force.

The general ambivalence in Britain to what was happening in South Africa during the spring of 1899 gradually turned to concern during the summer months, and by autumn into outright alarm. The *Mid Cumberland and North Westmorland Herald* feared the worst in its edition of 1st October:

With the mobilising of British troops to the Cape Colony, Westminster has clearly made its statement of intent. Moreover forces are being called upon from the Dominions of Australia, New Zealand and Canada for the good of the Empire… Although any hostilities will affect us little, we should be turning our attention to those who may, shortly, be risking their lives for the cause of freedom and democracy.

On October 9th, 1899, Kruger demanded the withdrawal of all British troops from the Transvaal frontiers within 48 hours, with the alternative of formal war. With the whole world watching, and the other European Empires — especially Germany — cheering for the little guy, Britain could not climb down.

✳ ✳ 4 ✳ ✳

In 1898, Dan Daley was enjoying his youth. He was 20 years old, he was now fully qualified as a joiner (earning 15s per week), he had his football and was still an active member of the Foresters Friendly Society. On 1st July 1898 his desire to broaden his horizons still further led him to join the Volunteer movement.

The volunteers were proposed in 1859, when the government recognised the need to have trained military personnel at home while their regular counterparts guarded its foreign dominions. The force would not therefore be enrolled for foreign service but for the protection of Hearths and Homes, their motto being 'Defence not Defiance.' Each Lord Lieutenant was invited to raise a Volunteer Corps in his county, so while Jacob Reed and Isaac Scott were slogging it out in India, back home eleven units of Volunteers were formed to protect Cumberland in their absence, while a further six units were formed in Westmorland.

Nationally the Volunteers soon became a type of club; their get-togethers were semi-social evenst, weekend drilling was light, and the crack amongst the lads was good. Subscriptions were levied from members, who also paid for their own uniforms and ammunition, while the government contributed to half the cost of the their arms. They found themselves figures of much amusement in the early days and when one group of local Rifle Volunteers ran to shelter from the rain so as not to spoil their uniforms, their reputation as harmless figures of fun was confirmed; in these days of innocence, SAS meant Saturdays and Sundays.

By the time Dan joined up things were a little more serious. The local Volunteer Battalions had officially become part of the Border Regiment a decade earlier and now in 1898, with training and drilling a serious business, reputation and standing among the population had improved immeasurably. A year later and the restriction on foreign service for the volunteers remained in place, but events in South Africa would soon reach crisis point and an urgent review of that edict would be required.

When the impatient, bellicose Sir Alfred Milner, the British High Commissioner, walked out of the Bloemfontein peace conference on 5 June 1899, he knew that he was casting the die that would almost certainly lead to war between the British-ruled states of Cape Colony and Natal, and their independent Boer neighbours in the Transvaal and Orange Free State. What Milner overlooked, however, was his army's low level of efficiency, and this state of unreadiness, coupled with the military capacity of the Boers and their determination to resist, spelled danger ahead for all.

On 16th September, Milner sent Colonial Secretary Joseph Chamberlain in London a request for 'speedy reinforcements of troops.' With the British Army numbering 250,000 regulars and 90,000 reservists, London decided to despatch troops from India. Among the reinforcements despatched directly to the Cape were the Border Regiment, who were in Malta on their way home from the subcontinent. The regiment numbered 26 officers and 1014 non-commissioned officers and men under the command of Colonel J. H. E. Hinde. On 27th September they boarded the *SS Sumatra* bound for the Cape.

So as the next month raced by, it was the Boer Presidents, Steyn and Kruger, who militarily found themselves in an advantageous position. This position was not lost on the two leaders who decided on a pre-emptive strike.

In a strange pre-war agreement, both sides decided that Bantu, Zulus and Swazis should be kept from joining either side; this was to be strictly a 'white man's war'.

The British were not the only ones to underestimate their opposition. As their enemy struggled to muster decent numbers on the ground, the Boers believed that they could be easily subdued, and with the threat of intervention from their European allies, most notably Germany, they felt that the British would back off, much as they did in 1881. The truth was that the Germans were happy to keep a watching brief, uncertain as they were about the opposition, the commitment needed, and the net benefits for them. Blind to German ambivalence, the Boers moved a force of 10,000 men to the Transvaal border with Natal on 10th October 1899. Their prime objective was to wipe out the British forces in the towns of Ladysmith, Dundee, Mafeking and Kimberly before the arrival of reinforcements. Safe in the knowledge that his men were in place President Paul Kruger issued his final ultimatum to the British:

> *Your British troops on the border of the Transvaal Republic must be instantly withdrawn. All British re-enforcements on the high seas must not be landed in any port of South Africa. If you fail to comply, within 48 hours the Transvaal will, with great regret, be compelled to regard your action as a formal declaration of war.*

Back home the British press had raised the stakes with its jingoistic reports: Queen and Empire, the enfranchisement of the uitlanders, and good old national pride were all trotted out as perfectly valid reasons for trouncing the Dutch upstarts. And the Colonies Minister, Joseph Chamberlain, by this time had changed his tune completely from his previously uncertain stance. He had formulated his lofty principles and justification for action by the war's outbreak, and within a week of hostilities commencing, he confidently informed the House of Commons:

> We are going to war in defence of principles – the principles on which this Empire has been founded, and upon which alone it can exist. The first principle is this – if we are to maintain our existence as a great power in South Africa, we are bound to show that we are both willing and able to protect British subjects everywhere when they are made to suffer from oppression and injustice. The second principle is that in the interests of the British Empire, Great Britain must retain the paramount Power in South Africa.

As Kruger was moving his men into position on 10th October, Private Dan Daley and his Penrith Volunteer colleagues 5,000 miles away were holding their regular shooting competition at the Troutbeck Ranges. No doubt military matters dominated talk amongst the men and particularly what their regular colleagues were up to in South Africa. Unknown to them at the time, the next twelve months were to prove a roller-coaster ride of excitement and danger.

The war officially began at five o'clock on Wednesday 11th October 1899, or as *The Times* put it with quintessential British-ness, '… just around tea time.' News of the commencement of hostilities reached Penrith on the 17th when the *Herald* reported the developments following Kruger's ultimatum that had been handed to a British agent in Pretoria. 'A piece of unwarranted insolence,' the paper quoted the agent's reply.

Within days the war was going badly for the British: the battles of Glencoe, Elandslaagte and Rietfontein had already been fought and lost. The Border Regiment landed in Cape Town on Saturday 20th October and was immediately ordered to Natal to bolster Sir George White's under-pressure army. Among their number was a Penrith lad, Private John Richardson, whose extracts from a letter home were printed in the *Penrith Observer* on 24th November and reflected the feeling among the men:

> It's as hot as India but the lads are in good spirits. We'll be going up country with Sir Redvers within the next few days. Hope to have things sorted out pretty quickly so we can get back home.

White was based at Ladysmith and had sent 40,000 of his troops to Dundee, 30 miles away, to guard the coalfields around the town. On 22nd October, under intense Boer pressure, the British troops had to flee Dundee, but in so doing they left behind some damning papers that the Boers passed on to a Reuters press officer, who wasted no time in wiring them round the world:

The papers unveil a thoroughly worked-out British scheme to attack the independence of both Boer Republics as far back as 1896, notwithstanding constant assurances of amity towards the Orange Free State.

This was the smoking gun the Boers (and the Germans) had been looking for. If there was any doubt before as to the intentions of the British Government, there certainly wasn't any now. The Boers went all out on the offensive. Within a fortnight, the situation looked very bleak for the British. Kimberly had been besieged within days of the commencement of hostilities and Mafeking quickly went the same way. From a military point of view both were fairly unimportant but Kimberly held a certain mystique with its diamond mines and more importantly still, British tycoon and imperialist Cecil Rhodes just happened to be there. In one of his less astute moments, Rhodes had mysteriously travelled to the town on 10th October, the day before war broke out.

But it was clear even at this early stage that the British simply didn't have enough manpower to cover the ground. The call went out to Empire in the motherland's hour of need. The Dominions responded admirably: Australia, New Zealand and Canada all sent men to supplement the depleted forces, as did Indian princes, and although the latter group were technically black men in this white man's war, they were our black men already, so that didn't really count.

Another group to sail south were journalists: special correspondents from all the national and quite a few provincial newspapers. If William Howard Russell had been the pioneer of the war correspondent, then by the time of the Boer War exponents of his profession appeared to be ten-a-penny. The press corps that went out to South Africa were in fact the prototype for today's endless teams of press and media who provide the blanket coverage of foreign conflicts which we now accept as the norm. The advantage they enjoyed over Russell was the use of new technology, including most notably, the telegraph. Back in Penrith, however, the *Herald* and the *Observer* relied upon the second-hand news from the likes of Reuters and the Press Association for their column inches.

By the end of October British troops started to pour into South Africa. Their Commander-in-Chief was General Sir Redvers Buller and his first task was to march north east to relieve Ladysmith and Kimberly, and in so doing halt the Boers' advance into (British) Natal and the northern Cape Colony. This first British offensive was to result in a catastrophe that would not only fail in its prime objective but would have far-reaching effects that would ultimately change British policy regarding further reinforcements.

Buller was highly thought of by his men, insisting on their receiving at least one hot meal a day, to include fresh meat and vegetables. Sadly, as far as his commanders were concerned, he was dogged by the buffoonery that had constantly hampered many a campaign throughout the century.

On 5th December Sir Redvers began his march north and by the 12th the British had reached the small town of Colenso. With the army travelled the battery of special correspondents who had sailed with the task force to cover the war. At Colenso, blocking the way to Ladysmith, were 4,500 Transvaalers. Much to the delight of the press corps, Buller prepared to engage the enemy on 15th December. W.H. Russell's tell-it-like-it-is style had, by 1899, evolved into colourful jingoism, intended to thrill and excite the eager public back home. The *Daily Telegraph* reporter, Bennett Burleigh, for example, sounded as though he was about to do himself a mischief as he reported on the British advance towards the imminent battle:

> *With death filling the air and tearing the ground, onward they went, the most superb spectacle of invincible manhood.*

The officers in khaki weren't much better: one of Buller's commanders, Colonel Charles Long, wasted no time in demonstrating his strategic ineptitude. Beforehand he told his men, 'Now the only way to smash these beggars is to rush in, straight at 'em.' He then proceeded to lead the guns of his Royal Artillery ahead of the advancing infantry. About 2,000 Boer rifles were waiting for him, and his men were cut to pieces. This typified the whole battle: Colenso was a disaster that had closely followed heavy defeats at Stormberg on 10th December and at Magersfontein the following day.

Another famous character present to report on the war and with a view to compiling a history of the conflict was Arthur Conan Doyle. It was Doyle who coined the phrase 'Black Week' when referring to the three defeats in that disastrous December period when the British lost almost 3,000 men, and his colleagues in the press quickly adopted this sound-bite as they raced to wire their reports back home.

In England the readers were appalled by the setbacks. How could the finest army on earth fail to defeat a bunch of ill-trained, ill-equipped, overweight Dutch farmers? There had already been a call to raise volunteer units for active service two months earlier as the war commenced, but wrapped up in their over-by-Christmas confidence, the War Office had baulked at this suggestion, unconvinced that enthusiastic amateurs could make a difference. Now, with 3,000 of their finest men lying dead 5,000 miles away and key towns under siege, their position was starting to soften.

On 18th December, as the call to arms grew in the press and on the street, the War Office announced that it would permit twelve battalions of militia and some 20,000 selected yeomanry to go to South Africa. The nation responded with a reinvigorated surge of expectation as tens of thousands of men flocked towards recruiting depots. The *Penrith Observer* carried the simple headline 'Volunteers called up to fight.' The Penrith Volunteers, like their counterparts elsewhere, responded enthusiastically to the news. The following day the *Observer* set out the strict criteria that each man would have to adhere to before he could be allowed to take up arms. He should be between the ages of 19 and 25, should be passed medically fit for action by army personnel, should be a first-class marksman and should preferably be unmarried. One young lad who fitted the bill perfectly was Dan Daley. Within eighteen months of his joining what was thought to be a semi-social group of part-time soldiers, he was now hoping to be selected for a major foreign military campaign.

✳✳ 5 ✳✳

As Christmas approached, the architects of the war were in disarray. Allowing volunteers to travel was hastily permitted and was one of eight measures intended to redress the course of the war. Others included appointing Lords Roberts and Kitchener in the roles of Commander-in-Chief and Chief of Staff respectively. Buller was, in effect, blamed for 'Black Week' and relieved of his command. Roberts and Kitchener were interesting choices as their characters could not have been more different: Roberts was a soldier's soldier, revered by his men who had grown up learning about his exploits in the Crimea and Afghanistan. Kitchener, on the other hand, was highly mistrusted due to his ruthless ambivalence to his men and the enemy alike. It was this odd couple then, that were despatched immediately to the Cape to assume command.

Dan Daley meanwhile was less concerned about the command structure and more with whether or not he would be selected as a member of the Volunteer Battalion. Two days after Christmas, as the 19th century drew to its close, Dan finally received the news he had been hoping for: he had been selected as one of seventeen Penrith Volunteers — under the command of Lieutenant John Francis Haswell — to join the regular battalion at the front. He was to be one of a hundred thousand from all sectors of society who were designed to swell the numbers of the army in South Africa (this was the forerunner of the patriotic fervour that inspired so many to volunteer in the First World War). In his history of the conflict, Arthur Conan Doyle reflected on the mood and the task facing those who stepped forward:

> It is one thing, however, to draw up paper reinforcements, and it is another, in a free country where no compulsion would be tolerated, to turn these plans into actual regiments and squadrons. But if there were any who doubted that this ancient nation still glowed with the spirit of its youth his fears must soon have passed away. For this far-distant war, a war of the unseen foe and of the murderous ambuscade, there were so many volunteers that the authorities were embarrassed by their numbers and their pertinacity. It was a stimulating sight to see those long queues of top-hatted, frock-coated young men who waited their turn for the orderly room with as much desperate anxiety as if hard fare, a veldt bed, and Boer bullets were all that life had that was worth the holding…Many could ride and not shoot, many could shoot and not ride, more candidates were rejected than were accepted, and yet in a very short time eight thousand men from every class were

wearing the grey coats and bandoliers.

The 3rd January 1900 edition of the *Penrith Observer* confirmed the names of the local men who were to represent the town in the Volunteer Battalion. The same edition carried the latest news from the front, and in particular an interesting article about a daring escape by a prisoner of war. Although it was only three days into the 20th century, by the end of the hundred years that lay ahead, the POW in question would be voted the Greatest Briton of all time by the present-day, media-inspired, competition-mad public.

Winston Churchill was already a well-known figure by the start of the war; he came from a famous family, he had fought in the Sudan less than two years earlier (charging with the 21st Lancers at the Battle of Omdurman) and in July 1899 he had contested — and lost — the parliamentary seat for Oldham. In mid-September, with the war imminent, Churchill cut a deal with the *Morning Post* to report on the war for £250 per month. He sailed for South Africa on 14th October, and on 15th November, barely a fortnight after his arrival, he managed to get himself captured by the Boers when the train he was travelling on was derailed whilst under heavy attack from Boers Kommandos. Following his escape he was given a hero's welcome when he got back to British lines and details were hurried back home for a much-needed good-news story. Such exposure catapulted Winston on to the world stage, where he was to remain for the rest of his life, and, of course, he revelled in it. Ever the showman, he didn't hesitate to add dramatic flair to his reports:

> *The long interval between the acts has come to an end. The warning bell has rung. Take your seats ladies and gentlemen…the curtain is about to rise.*

This fired up the British readers even more. Whatever the strength of public outrage after 'Black Week', they now had an unquenchable thirst for knowledge of the latest events in South Africa. Readers, both locally and nationally, began to gorge on the daily news as it filtered through from the army of correspondents. With the decision to allow Volunteers to bolster the regular forces at the front, both the *Mid Cumberland and North Westmorland Herald* (formerly the *Penrith Herald*) and the *Carlisle Journal* saw a sure-fire opportunity to grab their own piece of the action by appointing their own correspondents. The *Herald* had been founded by Thomas Hodgson; now, with Hodgson still on the board of directors that ran the newly renamed paper, he and his colleagues approached Joseph Harrison, one of the volunteers, to act as their reporter. Joe, from St Andrew's View in the town, was a good friend of Dan Daley as they had joined up together in 1898, and he agreed to keep a diary of his year in service and acquiesced to the paper printing a regular 'Leaves from my diary' column. The *Journal* similarly approached one of the Carlisle Volunteers, and Private Stephen Couling agreed to perform the same task for the city's readership.

On the evening of 15th January, Dan, Joe and their comrades were guests of honour at a concert given at The George Hotel in Penrith. The following day they were to start their odyssey by travelling to Carlisle for six weeks' training prior to embarking for South Africa. During the evening's event, one speaker made reference to the fact that the volunteers had often been laughed at and were subjected to many an unkind word; but now it was with great pride that the town sent these young men to serve their country. Each man was presented with a pipe and tobacco and informed that a collection made would be distributed among them on their troopship. It was the early hours before the evening ended and the men returned to their homes; as Dan Daley climbed into his bed that night, he knew that tomorrow would see the start of the greatest adventure of his young life.

Penrith on the morning of Tuesday 16th rekindled memories of the Jubilee festivities three years earlier: crowds lined the streets waiting to cheer their lads off, while businesses closed for the morning in anticipation of the impromptu parade. At 10 o'clock the men mustered in full dress uniform at the Drill Hall on Portland Place. Dan Daley stepped forward and signed up for one year's foreign service with No 1 Active Service Company of the Cumberland and Westmorland Volunteer Battalions of the Border Regiment. The crowd erupted into cheers as the men came out to be photographed, resplendent in their scarlet uniforms. Then, in double file, off they went towards the station, accompanied by the volunteers' band and that signature tune of the South African campaign, *Soldiers of the Queen*.

Through the cheering crowds and under the banner marked 'To Pretoria' they marched towards the packed station where the more sobering goodbye scene with friends and family was to take place. What Jane Daley said to her son — if any words could find their way past a choked throat in such circumstances — will never be known, but the thought of her youngest child going off to war must have been more than she could bear.

The following Saturday saw Private Harrison's first diary entry in the *Herald*. He reported the safe arrival in Carlisle and the subsequent medical examination; the forming of the whole Volunteer Battalion into the appropriate sections; and the commencement of drilling, skirmishing practice, kit inspections, and lectures on weaponry and disease. Whereas

The Penrith Volunteers in front of the Drill Hall in Portland Place, Penrith, with Dan Daley third from left in the back row. (Cumberland & Westmorland Herald)

some of the men were accommodated in the castle, Dan and Joe were among those in the relative luxury of the Viaduct Hotel.

The expedient to have these men trained up and shipped out could not have been greater as their regular colleagues in the field were taking a pounding. The Border Regiment had, during the first two weeks in January, marched towards Ladysmith to assist Buller (who, with the appointment of Roberts and Kitchener, had been reduced to commander in Natal only) in his second attempt to relieve the town. What was thought of as key to the Boers' defences was a 4,800-foot high mountain called Spion Kop. In the third week of January a battle for the hill took place: the Border Regiment lost heavily during the fighting (total British casualties were 1,740). When Private John Richardson wrote his letter home to Penrith, he relayed the optimism and high spirits felt by the men of Cumberland and Westmorland. After Spion Kop, another letter, written by Private Tommy Heyliss of Workington, gave an insight into the men's realisation of the task ahead and of the enemy they were facing:

> *We had seven days' fighting right off at a stroke, and our regiment lost very heavily. The first day we lost 121 men and we had hardly been twenty minutes in action, and the worst of it is that we cannot see where the Boers are firing from, because they are so deeply entrenched...Our good old Colonel [Hind] fell three times that I saw,*

and I heard him say: 'God bless you my lads; come on all.' Our regiment are sorry for him, as he was very well liked. We feel the want of him now. I do not know how many rank and file we lost but I know we lost over 200 men.

Another present at the battle was Winston Churchill. Revelling in his celebrity following his escape, the *Morning Post* was introducing him as 'the greatest correspondent of the day.' Moreover, Winston had now wangled himself a lieutenant's commission in the South African Light Horse (this despite the War Office forbidding such a duality of function). So Churchill both fought in and reported on the battle around the giant hill:

A fierce and furious shellfire was opened forthwith upon our troops. The shells were falling at the rate of seven or eight a minute and the shrapnel lashed the British troops. Dead and injured, smashed and broken by shells, littered the summit, until it was a bloody, reeking shambles. Corpses lay here and there; many of the wounds were of a horrible nature. To retreat; to flee down the hill would have been easy. It was not fear of punishment that held those who stayed and endured. A sense of duty, a fear of shame greater than that of physical fear, a sentiment that a man must not desert his comrades – these held through the long hours of the morning.

If this was Churchill's idea of the curtain rising on another dramatic act, it must have put the fear of God into Dan Daley and his colleagues who, while their regular colleagues were marching round Natal in temperatures of up to 100° Fahrenheit, were routemarching through the little snow-carpeted villages around Carlisle in sub-zero temperatures: Brunstock, Linstock, Rickerby and Crosby, or Wetheral Plains, Cumwhinton and Scotby all resounded to the sounds of the local volunteers' boots during those winter weeks. With a week to go before departure, Private Harrison's diary entry was reflective to the point of being chilling:

Sunday 25 February – Church parade, service in the Cathedral and dismissed. Some of the Penrith lads went home – perhaps for the last time in their life. Who knows? But we are in God's hands.

Dan was one of those lads that went home to see his mother and siblings before departure the following Saturday. What was said? What can be said in such circumstances? No doubt the hollow clichés: 'Keep your head down, son,' and: 'I'm sure it'll be fine,' were trotted out by loved ones, terrified at the prospect of the worst-case scenario. Whatever was said, Dan left Penrith and rejoined his colleagues in Carlisle on the Sunday night.

Finally, from the front, good news started to filter through: the sieges of Kimberley and Ladysmith had been relieved on 15th February and 28th February respectively. The news was greeted with a great outpouring of relief in Britain. Was this the start of the new act Churchill had been wittering on about the previous month? Private Dan Daley was about to find out first hand as, on Saturday 3rd March at 12.30 he marched out of the castle yard with the khaki-clad Volunteer Battalion to the strains of *Will ye no' come back again*, while the Carlisle crowd cheered their support. (This was the first war when khaki was universally issued as standard uniform. The idea of 'disguising' the uniforms originated from India where smocks and pyjamas were treated with a dye from a local dwarf palm to produce a drab yellow-green colour, known in Hindustani as khaki, or 'dust-coloured'.)

For some of the volunteers, their campaign was almost over before it had begun, when the over-enthusiastic throng of well-wishers caused a crush at the station. With a few of the soldiers having to be lifted on to the train, out of harm's way, their journey finally began. The mainline route was lined with people from all over Cumberland and Westmorland and they waved their support for each of the local lads from around the two counties.

At midnight, the *SS Nineveh* pulled out of Southampton harbour bound for the Cape. On board was the 1st Volunteer Active Service Company of the Border Regiment. The exhausting day came to an amusing end when Joe Harrison reported his colleagues' attempts to climb into their hammocks: 'It was a case of in one side and out the other.' Far tougher days were to lie ahead for the young part-timers.

✳ ✳ 6 ✳ ✳

What do you do if you are a soldier going to the front? What thoughts race through your mind in the solitary hours on board your transporter? Could there be a greater opportunity to confront the questioning of one's own mortality? Thank God the majority of us have never, and will never, be placed in such a position.

The officers in charge of the young volunteers on board the *SS Nineveh* kept their charges busy with parades on deck, physical exercise, sports contests between companies and arranging concerts for the men, given by regimental bands. In the 13th March edition of his 'Leaves From My Diary' column, Private Joseph Harrison entertained his Penrith readership with details of an afternoon sports event held on board ship the previous week. He recounted how he and Private Daley were chosen to represent their company in the rather innocent pastimes of egg and spoon, and potato races, and the rather more serious contest of cockfighting.

Cockfighting is an old nautical sport, enjoyed by sailors since before the Nelsonian period. It involves two opponents facing off in a six-foot ring with a stick fastened below their legs and securely bound hands. Each combatant then has to put his opponent either on his back or out of the ring. No doubt Jane Daley read with excitement about her son's exploits. Despite his being smaller than his opponent, the nimble and athletic Dan won his best of three bouts and found himself in the final. But young Daley's expedition was nearly cut short there and then, when he came up against Private Tommy Johnson. Tommy was a big lump of a lad from Staveley; twice the size of the Penrith joiner, he had already taken care of Dan's mate and our correspondent Joe Harrison in the previous round. Johnson proceeded to barge Dan around the deck of the *Nineveh* as if he was toying with a rag doll, no doubt to the cheering amusement of his colleagues. A lighter day than those ahead ended, 'with the men lathered in sweat as we crossed the equator.'

The Border lads helped to make up the number of 5,000 volunteers on the high seas heading for the Cape during March 1900. On land itself there were signs that the tide was beginning to turn against the Boers. On 17th March in the Orange Free State, its President Marthinus Steyn vacated his capital, Bloemfontein, as the British were starting to advance. They had already raised the sieges of Kimberly and Ladysmith and were turning their attention to the remaining garrison that had captured most attention in Britain from the very beginning: Mafeking. Mafeking was unheard of before the war, and was a small, strategically insignificant garrison as hostilities commenced. But that was soon to change when its British commander Colonel Robert Stephenson Smyth Baden-Powell immediately set the tone for the months ahead, and captured the imagination of Britons everywhere with his opening stiff-upper-lip despatch to the outside world from the besieged town: 'All well. Four hours' bombardment. One dog killed.' He continued to captivate the reading public for 217 days with his oddball witticisms and cricket analogies: '150 not out!' he proudly wired in February 1900.

Britain couldn't get enough of this eccentric and his beleaguered colleagues. The Boer War had all the captivation of a modern day World Cup campaign or an Olympic Games that has us sitting up to all hours to see how 'our lads' are doing. And if the war was becoming big box-office, then Baden-Powell was turning Mafeking into the blue riband event.

While the people of Penrith were feasting on news from all over South Africa, as well as being kept fully up to date by Private Harrison on the whereabouts of the local volunteers, the part-timers themselves were in the dark as to what the latest strategic position was regarding the war. 'We get no war news here,' lamented Joe Harrison as the volunteers headed for Port Elizabeth on 31st March. He and his colleagues finally disembarked on 9th April, and the following day joined up with their regular colleagues. Both parties appreciated the reunion; Harrison wrote, 'It was like being home again, meeting so many old friends in this foreign land.'

Such good days, however, were being far outnumbered by the bad for soldiers on the ground. The heat was beginning to take its toll on man and beast alike. As in the Crimea fifty years earlier, it became increasingly difficult to bury the dead, and animals were thrown into the nearest stream; an act that only succeeded in contaminating the river for miles, and as the marching soldiers filled their canteens with the poisoned water, so the disease cycle increased.

With the need for extra personnel the call went out for further units of volunteers throughout Britain. In Penrith, on 28th April, a reserve draft was ordered to report for active service. (Most of these would form part of the 2nd Volunteer Active Service Company despatched to the Cape the following year.) For the first time in British history, social classes other than the highest and the lowest were part of the fighting force. With Dan Daley and the 1st Active Service Company of volunteers were a chemist, a number of clerks, a photographer, a manservant, an insurance agent, a sweep, a French polisher and a whole host of men from rural and urban trades. The volunteers within the Border Regiment appeared to mix well with their regular colleagues and had the respect of their officers. But the same could not be said elsewhere, where volunteers complained about the treatment meted out by their superiors, and some officers found it difficult to handle the part-time soldier who had not been indoctrinated with the over-the-top, no-questions-asked mantra instilled into every regular.

As far as the lads from Cumberland and Westmorland were concerned, however, they were now part of the 1st Battalion of the Border Regiment, and were content, if a little footsore, with their lot. As part of General Arthur Fitzroy Hart's brigade (which included Brabant's Horse, New Zealanders, Kaffarian Rifles, the Royal Irish Rifles and the Somerset Regiment) the Borders began their long march towards the Transvaal border, within a week of volunteers landing in South Africa. Their first (and only) action came when the regiment reached Boschman's Kop on 21st April, where the Boers held position, barring the British advance. The following day, Hart ordered a dawn attack on the enemy positions.

The Boers occupied strong hill positions, with the main body of their force on a small dusty plateau, strongly fortified in front and on either side by stoutly constructed trenches. The starting pistol for this particular engagement came shortly after six o'clock with the exchange of artillery fire, before Hart gave the order for infantry to fan out and attack each of the enemy flanks. In his column for the *Carlisle Journal*, Private Stephen Couling of the Carlisle Company of Volunteers described what happened next:

> *The right half battalion of the Regiment were the firing line, while the left half (to which the Volunteers are attached) formed the supports. We advanced to within 500 yards of the enemy position. Then the supports were ordered to move up to the support of the firing line. We could plainly discern the mounted Boers and the artillerists with the enemy's guns. There was a river, which we successfully crossed under a heavy fire from the enemy, and obtained cover on the ridge of a hill on the right of the enemy. Our Company was steadily under a most galling fire and subjected to a strong cross fire from the crest of the plateau. While under cover a perfect storm of bullets passed over our heads, and many were the narrow escapes we had. The enemy had got the correct range and bullets and shells rained in our direction for fully two hours.*

Within the company of volunteers, all the Penrithians were known to be fighting shoulder to shoulder at this point. By the time they had circumnavigated the Boers' position, one of their number, Private Adam Irving, was shot in the face and Daley, Harrison and company dragged him to safety behind a stone wall under continuing heavy fire. Fighting continued throughout the day, until four o'clock in the afternoon, when the Boers finally retreated from their positions. When night fell, the exhausted soldiers bivouacked on the hills vacated by their enemy. Couling concluded, 'The night was very cold, but we had to endure the hardship. Supreme silence reigned, and no lights were allowed.'

The regiment's diary was a little more matter-of-fact about the encounter:

> The Border Regiment were ordered to attack the smaller kopjes lying at the foot of the hill, whilst the mounted troops under General Brabant turned the enemy's left flank. The Border Regiment successfully accomplished the task with slight loss, having only 7 men slightly wounded, of these one belonged to the Volunteer Company, who on this day had their first engagement with the enemy.

More marching followed for the Cumberland and Westmorland men before Private Harrison recorded their excitement at receiving their mails from home on 10th May. Mail from home has always been a great morale booster to the British soldier in the field and the volunteers found great solace in the much-needed lift. 'There was great jubilation seeing the good old *Herald*' reported Joe, as Dan and his mates ribbed him about his newfound fame. Private Harrison's morale quickly nose-dived however when a week later he was struck down with dysentery. The Penrith Volunteers had been inoculated against the germs of enteric fever (typhoid and paratyphoid) before they left home but avoiding some form of contamination was becoming virtually impossible in these extreme conditions.

Another lesson that had not been learned from the Crimea was that an unsanitary camp and inadequate hospitals could prove more fatal than the most determined foe. By the turn of the century Florence Nightingale and Mary Seacole had long since retired. Their legacy was the Army Nursing Service but its female compliment at the beginning of the war was still only one Lady Superintendent and 56 nursing sisters.

Two general hospitals and three private hospital units had been established by the middle of April 1900. Arthur Conan Doyle was not only a writer, he was also a doctor, and he actually emulated his literary creation, Dr John Watson, by serving in one of these field hospitals between April and June. He later wrote, 'We had neither beds nor utensils enough to treat such a number properly.' As conflicting rumours about the medical facilities filtered back to Britain, *The Times* despatched yet another special correspondent out to review conditions. W. L. A. B Burdett-Coutts was also a Member of Parliament and what he found shocked the nation:

> *Men were dying like flies for want of adequate attention…On that night (Saturday 28th April 1900) hundreds of men were lying in the worst stages of typhoid, with only a blanket and a thin waterproof sheet between their aching bodies and the hard ground, with no milk, hardly any medicines, without beds, stretchers, or mattresses, without pillows, without linen of any kind, without a single nurse amongst them, with only a few private soldiers acting as 'orderlies', rough and utterly untrained for nursing and with only three doctors to attend on 350 patients.*

There was an outcry in Britain. Had we learned nothing from the Crimean debacle? By the time the matter was debated in Parliament, and a Royal Commission despatched (in August) to conduct a formal enquiry, the worst months of May and June were over.

Interestingly, in his despatches from his hospital bed Private Harrison reported seeing Miss Rhodes (Cecil's sister) on several occasions. 'She takes a great interest in the welfare of the soldiers,' wrote Joe. Meanwhile, Private Daley marched on with his regiment into the town of Wepener, fifteen miles on from Boschman's Kop, to the strains of the Regimental March *John Peel*, and much to the delight of the inhabitants, many of whom were emigrant Cumberland miners. From there the Border Regiment (with the Fusilier Brigade and the Dublin Fusiliers) travelled by rail to the strategically important Fourteen Streams, and then marched the 26 miles to cross the border into the Transvaal, the first British troops to do so.

Special mention of the men's efforts was made on behalf of General Hart himself, although instead of a genuine 'well done lads', it was in blustering fashion that so characterises the British Army:

> *As far as he can arrive at the tolerably correct estimate of the ground covered, these two battalions in the course of last night marched 26 miles in the space of 19 hours including all stops and rests, and the strong point of it is that they did it in such a good style that they arrived at the end of it in compact formation while going at a good pace and with no straggling or falling out. The Major General will accordingly put this march on record.*

Two hundred miles away, across the South African veldt, Colonel Robert Stephenson Smyth Baden-Powell was still rallying his beleaguered garrison at Mafeking, while relieving British forces continued their inexorable march towards it. In Britain, the public held its breath, as if captivated by an unmissable sporting event, hoping against hope that the town could be successfully retaken. Then on 17th May 1900, Mafeking was relieved. The following night at 9.17 pm, the Reuters News Agency in London received a message from its correspondent in Pretoria, who confirmed the Transvaal government had officially abandoned the siege. London went wild: this was Jonny Wilkinson's drop goal, Steve Redgrave's fifth gold medal and Geoff Hurst's hat-trick (with some people on the pitch) all rolled into one. As news was wired round the country, the capital's delirious excitement was mirrored throughout. In Newcastle, rockets were sent into the night sky, while in Glasgow all the church bells were rung.

In Penrith, news was received from Liverpool at 9.45 pm and the editor of the *Penrith Observer* wasted no time in posting the news in the office's window. A crowd quickly gathered and news spread round the town like wildfire. A barrel was filled with shavings and set alight in King Street. Bell-ringers from St Andrew's Church were hastily summoned and peeled their delight until well after midnight. Singing, music, cheering all continued until two o'clock in the morning when the crowd finally dispersed. Early next morning Penrithians hung out their old Jubilee flags while the bands played in Crown Square and King Street. The council declared a holiday for the following Thursday. More than a few people were on the street; they thought it was all over. They were to be sadly mistaken.

✳ ✳ 7 ✳ ✳

So then, the war was over: Lord Roberts had reported as much to London. By the time Mafeking had been relieved, Kimberly and Ladysmith were already in the bag; before the month was out, Johannesburg and her gold mines were to be secured; and Presidents Steyn and Kruger had fled their capitals of Bloemfontein and Pretoria, respectively. Job done.

The celebrations that marked the relief of Mafeking would surely double up as an end to the war—a kind of Victory in South Africa Day. Arthur Conan Doyle packed up his medical kit and raced back to England to complete what he thought was to be the last chapter of his epic history of the war (little did he know it at the time but he was destined to add a further nine chapters to his work). London wasted no time in sending the word round the Empire that the Boers had been defeated. There is no question that the tide had irrevocably turned Britain's way by summer 1900, but no one anticipated what the Boers chose to do next. Instead of surrendering, as they were supposed to do, the fighting men adopted guerrilla tactics in order to disrupt the British occupation of their country.

The powers in Westminster certainly knew how to talk the talk, but the ordinary troops on the ground in South Africa were wracked with self-doubt and despair. The war was proving unglamorous for the British soldier: he was puzzled by the Boer tactics and appearance, constantly wrong-footed by the unorthodox method of fighting and frustrated that this most stubborn of enemies couldn't be put away; there were no heroic battles, just the monotonous foot slogging against this invisible enemy. To those soldiers tramping the veldt, this all now seemed quite pointless.

This 'guerrilla phase' of the war started almost unnoticed by the British. While everyone was basking in the glory of victory back home, Boer Kommandos had begun their hit-and-run tactics as early as the spring of 1900. By midsummer these skilled equestrian marksmen were causing havoc amongst the British troops, who were reduced to marching across the veldt to occupy key cities vacated by the Boer governments. No sooner had Roberts entered Pretoria on 5th June, than two days later a Boer general (C. R. de Wet) captured British supplies worth £500,000 at Roodewal. Extra troops were to be ordered to Pretoria.

It was now the middle of June 1900 and the Border Regiment were among those ordered to the Transvaal capital. Private Joe Harrison was still in hospital with dysentery. Dan Daley and the rest of the volunteers, along with their regular colleagues, already with with 200 miles of marching behind them, prepared for the long slog ahead. Notwithstanding the British victories, the spirits among the men were starting to drop: hot days, cold nights, the dusty open veldt and waist-deep swamps only succeeded in sapping morale and rotting boots and uniform. When Corporal Bill Carter from Maryport picked up his pen to write home, he wasn't interested in any brave-faced rhetoric:

> You'll be wondering when you are going to hear from me again, but opportunities for writing seldom occur when on the march. We are camped here ten miles from Pretoria waiting for orders. We are in the most degenerate state of unpicturesque vagrancy, worn out boots and clothing, men unkempt, dirty and rarely washed, subsisting on a bare ration that never satisfies the appetite in a part of the world that never evolved beyond the first stage of creation, a bare, desolate, cheerless place where you can never buy, beg or steal anything eatable. I've devoured my day's allowance of biscuits for my breakfast, and must trust to anticipation to allay the appetite. I'm now smoking a raking up of my pockets – tobacco dust, biscuit dust, and shreds of khaki, not a very fragrant mixture but better than nothing. Closing as I am at the end of my paper with love to all and hoping to be home soon, for 'hope springs eternal in the human breast,' and hunger infernal reigns in the human stomach. We've been tramping the Transvaal under General Hunter. It's bitterly cold at night with a cruel keen wind that pierces through one like the point of a dagger. How much longer is this confounded war going to last? I'm not 30, yet I look 40 and feel 46. I assure you that often with many others I've prayed to be knocked over. If it's fatal, you're finished. If it's simply a wound, you enjoy all the comforts of hospital. I'm as thin a cigarette paper and about as vigorous as a centenarian! Yours affectionately, William the famishing.

Finally, the regiment entered the Transvaal capital on 13th July. Pretoria was a pretty little city in its own right. After the journey the Border lads had undertaken, its picturesque red and blue rooftops, with the occasional church spire peeping out from amongst the masses of trees and colourful shrubbery, must have appeared like Eden itself. The troops were tired, grimy and footsore, but they felt they had at last reached their destination, the end of a very long road. Private Daley and his colleagues had marched 360 miles from 15th April; if he had wondered why he had been tramping round Wreay, Wetheral and Dalston in the snow, only six months earlier, he now knew the reason.

While Dan finally enjoyed some well-earned rest and recuperation in Pretoria (he even managed to pen a few lines to his mother to that effect), elsewhere in both the Transvaal and the Orange Free State, Boer guerrillas were causing havoc amongst the invading forces. Although the major cities were now secured, the small villages and homesteads remained virtually untouched by British hands. Why wouldn't they be? The people there couldn't muster large organised regiments that could trouble the British Army. What they could, and did, do however, was to provide shelter for the Boer Kommandos: they were hijacking British troops, stealing supplies and then blending into the small town environment, undetectable by their enemy. The British had to tackle this problem and deny the Boers movement. When the Kommandos started seizing mail trains in order to deny the ordinary soldier his morale-boosting news from home, it was described by the soon-to-depart Arthur Conan Doyle as 'unsporting'. If the Boers were unsporting with their tactics, then the British were about to become barbaric with theirs.

Records of the first farm burnings are dated around March 1900, but by midsummer, Roberts and Kitchener decided to up the ante by razing as many homesteads as possible, in order to discourage people from aiding and abetting active Kommandos. This scorched-earth policy was to be supported by the building of 8,000 blockhouses across the two countries (a little like the milecastles along Hadrian's Wall) interspersed with 3,800 miles of barbed wire fencing. This, it was hoped, would virtually hem in the enemy and seal victory.

The Border Regiment were soon on the march again in August under General Clements, initially north to Kommando Nek and then further west to Crocodile River, where they prepared to attack an enemy stronghold. The regular troops left the volunteers to guard the camp, while they went hunting for Boers. It was at this point that Private Joe Harrison returned to his company after his long illness. 'All the Penrith lads are doing well,' he reported back to the *Herald* on 11th September. Duties for Harrison, Daley et al consisted of four-hour lookouts for Boer Kommandos. Harrison sounded as though he was on safari at one point, referring to the various forms of wildlife to be seen, and evidence of the strain on the concentration of the men was let slip when he recorded on 12th September that there was good fishing in Crocodile River and he spent time watching the 'exotically coloured birds!' On the same day the regulars of the regiment skirmished with the enemy at Boschfontein, successfully scattering the Boers from the surrounding area, before rejoining their part-time colleagues. The regimental diary records the distance marched by the Borders from the point at which the volunteers joined the regulars in April:

Relief of Wepener	170	m i l e s
From Vryburg (May 30) to Pretoria (July 12)	360	"
With General Ian Hamilton	430	"
With General Clements up to date	370	"

It also stated that it was now time for the volunteers to leave the regulars. Joe Harrison jumped to the conclusion that he and his mates would be going home, as he wired back to Penrith, 'This is a preliminary step for home.' The volunteers paraded at two o'clock on the afternoon of 6th October and were inspected by Major Pelley, an event that was captured by the camera of one of the Border Officers. The Major thanked the men for their assistance during their time with the regiment and gave orders to prepare to march back to Pretoria the following day. Joining the volunteers from the Yorkshire Light Infantry, the Worcesters, and the 2nd Northumberland, the Borders escorted a convoy of 40 Boer prisoners on Sunday 7th October to their capital. The truth, apparently unknown to the men themselves, was that they were not taking their first steps home to Cumberland, but they were about to put their civilian skills to the test, as help was needed in fortifying the north of the country.

Upon receipt of Harrison's latest despatch, confusion and excitement jostled one another in Penrith as the townsfolk tried to establish confirmation as to whether or not their lads were homeward bound. The uncertainty was exacerbated when, on 20th October, the *Herald* printed a telegram sent by Penrith's own Lieutenant Haswell to his wife that simply read, 'Pretoria Company coming home.'

At the same time in South Africa the farm burning was in full swing. Despite many of his officers feeling badly about leaving women and children to be turned out on to the veldt with no means of support as their homes were razed, Kitchener would not be swayed from such an extreme measure. When a solution was finally found for the thousands of homeless families, it proved to be as controversial as the farm-burning itself. Camps were built to house the homeless; it was thought to be a humanitarian gesture as the occupants would be fed and kept safe from any fighting. The press however, were soon on to the story and news of the disease-ridden camps housing the Boer civilians, the first of whom quickly started to perish under the British gross mismanagement, began to filter back to England. This war was starting to leave a sour taste in the mouth of the British public who were beginning to feel uneasy about stories involving the deaths of women and children under British authority. To head off any adverse

The inspection of the volunteers on their departure from the regular battalion

feeling towards the ordinary soldier, Lord Roberts penned an open letter to the British public that was printed in one of the Penrith newspapers on 10th November:

> *Lord Roberts and his army — An appeal to the public dated 30th September 1900. Hope you welcome the soldiers who have been so magnificent in their efforts. I want to dispel the scurrilous rumours about the men's misbehaviour. These are malicious falsehoods and I hope there will be nothing to mar the homecoming.*

For the Penrith Volunteers, there was to be no homecoming. They were to proceed up country and work on building blockhouses, designed to cut off the mobile Boer Kommandos. As for the Boer women and children, they continued to suffer the burning of their farms and confinement to the camps. Like all bright ideas of the day, the camp policy hadn't properly been thought through. In reality it threatened to wipe out the Boer population. There was not enough money to develop the camps properly; they became full to overflowing, and the odd weak child, dying, was fast becoming scores — hundreds — of families perishing every day. By the end of the war the number of deaths in the camps was estimated at 30,000. And in an ironic twist, the name invented by the British for these establishments would come back to haunt them forty years later: the watching Germans noted that they called them concentration camps.

✳ ✳ 8 ✳ ✳

Windy all day, and at 11 o'clock a cyclone struck. Several tents were blown down, the officers' mess tent among the number, and the whole place was smothered about four or five inches thick with sand. The strangest thing about it was that Dan Daley and I had a small bivouac pitched right where the full force of the wind was, and within six or seven yards of the officers' mess tent, and it stood the strain like a Trojan, never budging an inch. We were about smothered with the sand, and as one end of our bivouac was open it came in, in bucketfuls. Although it was rough it was all over in about ten minutes. One officer who came for his servant passed the following quaint remark when I said to him that it was rather rough: 'Well, if we haven't bled for our country by [...] we have suffered.'

Private Harrison's report on 12th October was light-hearted enough. While he and Dan chuckled at their colleagues' misfortune, their families in Penrith waited for confirmation of their return. But days turned to weeks and finally when news did come, it wasn't to inform the *Herald's* readership of the volunteers' pending return; it was, in fact, to inform them of the part-timers' orders to move up-country to build a blockhouse near Kroonstadt, some thirty miles north of Pretoria.

Daley and Harrison tramped on, as this monotonous 'war' showed no signs of ending. Morale ebbed and flowed: when they arrived at Kroonstadt, Dan and Joe struck lucky again as they found themselves billeted in a vacated miner's hut with 'spring mattresses and bedsteads' (Harrison also reported, quite matter-of-factly, that the two 'made ourselves very comfortable by doing as the rest did, going in for a bit of looting'.) It wasn't long before morale started to drop again, however; Joe wrote of the first three days of November 1900: 'Three of the most miserable days that a human being ever put in—rain, rain and more rain.'

If the war was becoming a dreary, tedious drag for the soldiers on the ground in South Africa, in London it was becoming an embarrassing inconvenience. And if the powers-that-be were feeling a growing discomfort at the unexpected elongation of the conflict, then the appearance of a British woman called Emily Hobhouse into the fray was to cause havoc in the press and Parliament alike. Hobhouse was a social worker, who travelled to South Africa (a la Mary Seacole) to see for herself the terrible conditions suffered by the Boer women and children in the

162

concentration camps. In Britain the public had hitherto turned a blind eye to the concentration camps, but now the attention drawn to them by Emily's revelations became explosive.

Their consciences pricked by printing stories of starving Boer babies, journalists now rushed to denounce imperialism. In the House of Commons, the 'Welsh wizard' of the Liberal Party, David Lloyd George, grilled the government on the horrors of the camps in South Africa:

> *A war of annexation, against a proud people must be a war of extermination, and that is unfortunately what we are committing ourselves to. Burning homesteads and turning women and children out of their homes. The savagery that follows will stain the name of this country.*

Fellow-Liberal and future prime minister Henry Campbell-Bannerman would later (and extremely controversially) describe Kitchener's policy in South Africa as 'barbaric'. The Liberals argued that imperialism wasn't just immoral; it was a rip-off, paid for by the majority of the British people, but benefiting a tiny number of 'fat cats'.

As controversy raged in Britain, the oblivious volunteers of the Border Regiment continued to patrol and fortify the veldt 5,000 miles away. Some light relief came in the middle of November when Private Harrison switched from war reporter to sports reporter, as he gave details of a football match held between the Border Volunteers and their counterparts from the Royal Fusiliers. Dan Daley was picked to play up front for the local lads. Joe takes up the story:

> *The Borders kicked off against a strong wind, and at once pressed but were unable to score. Daley, Harris and Slack played a grand game. Dan Daley at centre was the pick of the teams and had very hard lines in not scoring. At half time the game came to an abrupt conclusion through a terrific thunderstorm that broke right over us and drenched players and spectators alike. I think the Border team would have won if the game had finished as the Fusiliers were about 'pumped out'.*

Such all-too-brief respite from the day-to-day drudgery must come as a great relief to any soldier; the only thing Dan had to worry about that day was the Royal Fusiliers' offside trap. Elsewhere, throughout the country, the Boers continued to set traps of a different sort; their guerrilla strikes were countered by more farm-burning, and together these two tactics threatened to prolong the conflict indefinitely. Christmas came and went for the volunteers, with nothing to break the monotony other than garrison sports days and cricket matches.

The volunteers' blockhouse

Private Harrison reported that 'all the Penrith lads are keeping well and are pretty anxious to get home' on 5th January, and wrote of the sadness of the troops at hearing of the death of 'the good old Queen' on the 24th. Then on Friday 7th February, Harrison wrote a significant piece that caught the attention of the Daleys of Stricklandgate, Penrith: 'Nothing much of interest transpired. Dan Daley had to go into hospital but is doing fairly well.' Despite subsequent correspondence to the effect that Dan was 'progressing favourably,' the worry caused to Jane Daley and her family should not be understated, given the horror stories that had been graphically detailed in the press, of death and disease in the hospitals of South Africa.

By the end of the war, 28,000 British soldiers would be dead, with three-quarters perishing from diseases such as typhoid, dysentery and the dreaded enteric fever. Several men from the Volunteer Active Service Company of the Border Regiment succumbed to this killer. As far as Dan was concerned, he had contracted malaria and the Kroonstadt hospital was his billet for the following six weeks, while his colleagues completed their building of the blockhouse at the same location. Jane sent her son a parcel: chocolate, notes of best wishes and the odd item of clothing from home, aiding the recovery of the stricken soldier. Daley was back with his colleagues by the end of March, just in time to receive the best news of all: the volunteers were finally to go home. Sadly for one of Dan's Penrith colleagues, Private Taylor, who was also suffering from malaria, he was not fit enough to travel home and had to be left behind in Kroonstadt Hospital.

There was one last photo opportunity for the men in front of their blockhouse before embarking on the *SS Tagus* at Cape Town on 9th April.

The Penrith Volunteers marching through Middlegate
(Cumberland & Westmorland Herald)

Twenty days later they disembarked and prepared for the final leg of their [train] journey home. The conflict still rumbled on in South Africa, but the volunteers had done their twelve months' service and it was the last thing on their minds, as it was for the people in the towns and villages around Cumberland and Westmorland, as they prepared for the grand homecoming. Penrith was representative of the excitement that ran throughout both counties: tradesmen decorated their shops and council officials ordered bunting and flags to be hung across the street, while the townsfolk dug out their jubilee union flags once more to drape them from upper floor windows.

The men themselves experienced a hors d'oeuvre to their own personal celebrations when they arrived in Carlisle after travelling through the night from Southampton. Carlisle folk turned out in their thousands at eight o'clock in the morning to see the first Border Regiment soldiers return from a war they had been experiencing through the dramatic press reports of such contrasting figures as Private Stephen Couling and Winston Churchill. The euphoria felt by the non-Carlisle men must have been tinged with a little frustration as the formalities that befit such an occasion were played out. Through the flag-waving crowd, the men marched to the drill hall for inspection, attended a smoking concert, given in their honour (at nine in the

*Two views of Devonshire Street as the volunteers return home
(Cumberland & Westmorland Herald)*

morning!), marched to the town hall where Mayor Hurst thanked them for their efforts before a thanksgiving service was held in the cathedral. Finally, a short march to the castle, where commanding officer Colonel Bind inspected them and presented them all with a souvenir card from Cape Town, before being allowed to fall out.

The Penrith and Kendal lads made their way to the station for the eleven-thirty train south. What went through Dan Daley's mind (or the mind of any soldier returning from a war, for that matter) can only be guessed at. Joe Harrison wrote that the hardships and discomforts of the previous twelve months were forgotten as the men approached Penrith. Throughout the town itself, a pre-arranged siren from the gas works shrieked their imminent arrival. The *Herald* recorded that, 'at eight minutes past twelve precisely' the train carrying the men came into view amid a crescendo of foghorns, ringing cheers and waving hats, that were countered by the sight of khaki-clad arms waving pith helmets and slouch hats from the windows of the train. On the platform, as the locomotive ground to a halt, feet shuffled and necks craned, as friends and family strained to catch sight of a son, a brother, a husband. If Dan had left twelve months earlier to his mother's tears of apprehension, the floods of relief and joy that greeted him could not have been more different.

When the 'private' welcomes were over, it was time for the sixteen heroes to set foot on the streets of the their home town for the first time in over twelve months. As they appeared at the station entrance, they were greeted by a wall of noise, emanating from the thousands of Penrithians who had gathered to pay homage. The volunteers who had not been selected for active service escorted their colleagues into the town through the cheering crowd. Dan Daley had taken part in a similar procession four years earlier in honour of the Queen; now it was he who was the centre of the town's attention, as it took thirty minutes for the South Africa veterans to pick their way through King Street towards Market Square. In Devonshire Street, the vast crowd gathered around the monument, while others could be seen hanging from windows. The statutory policeman on his white horse marshalled the throng, as the men gathered under the balcony of the Liverpool Bank (now Barclays), prior to the town's dignitaries giving speeches from the first floor window above. The men each received an inscribed gold watch from the people of the town, before the national anthem again resounded through the streets of Penrith and they were allowed to go home. For young Daley, one task remained: he rejoined his active service colleagues at the home of their commanding officer Lieutenant Haswell, where a small reception was held and a final

The volunteers at Lt. Haswell's home on the day they returned to Penrith with Dan Daley second from the right on the front row and Joe Harrison on the extreme left of the front row.

photograph was taken on the lawn outside. Dan's adventure of a lifetime was finally over; it was now time to settle down to a quiet life.

✳ ✳ 9 ✳ ✳

Of course, the war rumbled on. In fact, while Dan was trying to settle back into some sort of normality, a 2nd Active Service unit of volunteers left Cumberland and Westmorland in June 1901 for their twelve-month stint. But alas for those men (and those regulars who were still in South Africa) the people in Britain, other than family members, had no further interest in this dirty war. In March 1901 the first overtures for peace had failed because the Boer leaders steadfastly refused to give up their countries' independence. Their determined resistance had led to worldwide sympathy, and the ever-watchful Germans were even making bellicose overtures about joining the conflict on the side of the Afrikaners.

In a straw-clutching effort to placate his enemy and any potential allies, the idiotic Kitchener even resorted to trying, and convicting, three Australian officers for allegedly shooting Boer prisoners-of-war, and two of the officers, Lieutenants Harry 'Breaker' Morant and Peter Hancock, were executed. Such nonsense only discredited the British still further.

So by March 1902, even with the eventual outcome of the war — due to sheer weight of numbers — in little doubt, the British were desperate to force an end game; continued (if greatly diminishing) guerrilla attacks and the agonies of the concentration camps were unnecessarily draining resources, shattering the image of Empire and needlessly prolonging a result which was inevitable.

The Boers too had been ground down until even this most stubborn of foes began to realise that continued resistance was futile. Boer leaders felt it right and proper that if any negotiating was to be done, elected representatives of the different [remaining] Kommando units should be given the opportunity of discussing terms that might ultimately lead to the sacrifice of their independence. So when the British proposed a peace conference on 23rd March 1902, sixty representatives of the said units turned up at Pretoria to negotiate.

For two months much huffing and puffing took place before finally, a little before midnight on 31st May, the two parties signed the peace treaty of Vereening at Melrose House in Pretoria. The proud Boers voted 54 to 6 to surrender their independence to the British and recognise the authority of King Edward VII in exchange for seven concessions that seemed fairly irrelevant at the time (anything to get this damn war over with). They included repatriating prisoners of war, protection of the Afrikaans language in schools and law courts, and various economic safeguards, such as the maintenance of property rights. The most significant and far-reaching concession to the Boers, however, was the agreement to the disenfranchisement of all black people. Unknown to those at the time, the first seeds of apartheid had been sown.

But for now, all that mattered was that the war was finally over. The news sprinted across the world's communication wires. At three minutes to seven in the evening on Monday 2nd June, the *Penrith Observer* received two telegrams simultaneously, one from the *Daily Express* and one from the Press Association advising the town of the news. As details spread around the streets, an announcement was made in St Andrew's; bells rang, flags flew, people gathered. But there was not the same outpouring of jubilation that greeted the relief of Mafeking; more a collective sigh of relief that the conflict in that far away place, with its funny sounding names, would no longer take up the print space in the local papers.

The Border Regiment returned home shortly after the peace declaration: the campaign had witnessed them march 2,000 miles and suffer over a thousand casualties. In total, Britain lost 28,000 soldiers, while their South African opponents lost about 4,000 troops as well as over 25,000 civilians who died in the concentration camps. 12,000 black Africans also died, either in the concentration camps or through serving as non-combatant auxiliaries on both sides (so much for the white man's war).

Some modern historians feel it is worth debating who actually won and who lost the Boer War, such was the crippling cost to Britain both in humanitarian and financial terms. Militarily, a quarter of a billion pounds was serious money in those days. The South African conflict was almost to Britain what Vietnam would be to America and Afghanistan would be to Russia later in the century. Controversy raged at the time also; the Colonial Secretary, Joseph Chamberlain, was publicly accused of profiting from the war, as allegations of sleaze ran through the Palace of Westminster.

As for Dan Daley, he resumed his small-town existence, living with his mother on Stricklandgate, Penrith, and working as a joiner, in maintenance, at the Middlegate Brewery on the street of the same name. Thacka Beck flows under Penrith and in the late 19th and early 20th century was the main water supply to the town. The brewery operated until 1910, when it was pulled down to make room for the Alhambra Theatre, which still stands today as a cinema. While the 2nd Active Service unit of volunteers were in South Africa, Dan and his 1st unit colleagues were invited to Manchester to receive their campaign medals from Lord Roberts, in October 1901.

Reaching Manchester at eleven o'clock on Wednesday 9th October, the men were formed up in alphabetical order and marched to Hulme Barracks. Private Stephen Couling, the special correspondent in South Africa for the *Carlisle Journal*, resumed his duties for the event:

> *With military punctuality the proceedings opened at 14.00. The Commander-in-Chief with a brilliant staff of officers entered the building under the Royal Box, which occupied the central position, and was received with tremendous cheering. The working of presenting the medals was at once undertaken by Lord Roberts. The medals were in cardboard packets, and almost as fast as the Volunteers could walk to and past the Commander-in-Chief their rewards were handed to them and they marched out of the arena. As the first man approached the Field-Marshal, the band of the 2nd Life Guards struck up the Soldier's Chorus from Faust.*

Once the ceremony was over, the men departed Manchester at 5.45pm. The following day, further celebrations took place after the Penrith Volunteers had returned home, during which one final presentation was made: the *Herald* presented Joe Harrison with a walnut desk for his sterling efforts with his 'Leaves from my Diary' column. The brass plaque was inscribed, 'From the editor of the Herald to Mr. J. W. Harrison as a small appreciation of valuable services rendered as correspondent with the serving Volunteer Company, the Border Regiment during the South Africa Campaign 1900-1901.' And that was that: the fifteen minutes of fame enjoyed by Dan, Joe and their mates were over. As the war petered out in the summer of 1902, the volunteers reverted to their part-time duties: weekend training and the odd parade, while Penrith settled back into its sleepy, provincial existence.

In Westminster post-war finger pointing continued as controversy over the conflict continued. In South Africa, meanwhile, one of the chief architects of the war, Sir Alfred Milner, was setting about securing the peace between the British and the Boers by developing a policy of conciliation. Sadly, in order to achieve this, a third party was identified as a common enemy: the black Africans. In a speech in Johannesburg, Milner blatantly asserted:

> *... the white man must rule, because he is elevated by many, many steps above the black man; steps which will take the latter many centuries to climb, and which it is quite possible that the vast bulk of the black population will never be able to climb at all.*

Would this sorry business ever end? Britain and Empire was in desperate need of a good-news story in early 1903, and the best that could

*The unveiling ceremony of the South Africa War Memorial in Penrith
(Cumberland & Westmorland Herald)*

be mustered came on 10th March, when King Edward and Queen Alexandra celebrated their 40th wedding anniversary. Great play was made in the press of festivities and celebration (although the King could hardly be described as the bastion of fidelity and domesticity!)

Two days earlier, on 8th March 1903, Dan Daley had made his own entrance into the greatest institution of them all. The previous year he had begun to court Alice Rylands, the youngest of William and Matilda Rylands' eight children, who were fellow parishioners at St Catherine's Church. On a lovely spring morning the two were married at the church in front of friends and family. Later that year, Dan's happiness was complete when his son John was born, on 7th September. (It is unknown whether John was premature or not!) The only negative for the young family was their inability to afford their own house, so the ever-patient and accommodating Jane Daley once again provided the space at her home on Stricklandgate for son, daughter-in-law and grandson.

Dan's job was a relatively secure one, although employment throughout post-war Britain was at best tenuous, as the national economy struggled to regain momentum. Forty per cent of Britons lived in cities of more than 100,000 inhabitants at this time, and the trading world was now less favourable to industries traditionally dominated by British exports such a coal, textiles and heavy engineering. For the majority of skilled workers, however, life was more favourable than that of their unskilled contemporaries. Diet, health and housing had all improved in the final quarter of the 19th century and in 1900 a Labour Representation Committee was established, to speak for the ordinary worker. Six years later it changed its name to the Labour party.

Life for those in the villages and small towns was much simpler: work, church and leisure activities filled their time and the sense of community in the close-knit environment brought a general feeling of togetherness and well-being. Leisure activities were normally organised through local clubs for local people, but Penrith wasn't averse to staking a claim to the odd national event either. On Friday 16th September 1904, for example, the town virtually closed down to welcome William Frederick Cody—aka Buffalo Bill—and his Wild West show. Schools and businesses closed as thousands of families flocked to Foundry Field to witness the spectacle. Three special trains transported 500 horses and 800 people to Penrith. On that late summer's afternoon, Dan, Alice and baby John witnessed the world famous Buffalo Bill and his troupe bucking broncos, lassoing cattle, and re-enacting the Battle of the Little Big Horn and Custer's Last Stand.

Cody performed hundreds of shows throughout North America and

Europe between 1883 and 1906. His Penrith show was part of a four-year European tour, 1902-1906. Cody single-handedly cleaned up the shoddy image of the Wild West with these shows and influenced thousands of European children and their descendents (your author among them!) by beginning the mythological image of Cowboys and Indians that still survives today.

On the national and international stage, cowboys of another sort were still trying to rectify the blunders made before and during the disastrous war. Diplomatic changes were needed as Britain sought to re-structure her foreign policy by brokering an alliance with Japan and developing the entente cordiale with France. Militarily, the Committee of Imperial Defence was established in the aftermath of the war and after two years' worth of commissions, reviews and inquiries about the conflict, sweeping military and organisational changes were recommended.

One of the options being explored in this belt-tightening, post-war, economy-drive age was the reduction in the numbers of volunteers. Throughout the spring and early summer of 1905, rumours abounded that defence cuts were to be made and that the part-timers were for the chop. Finally, in July, all commanding officers throughout the country received instruction to reduce numbers of volunteers after stringent medical examinations of the all men. There was a firestorm of protest in the provincial press, who were quick to point out the work done by the men during the war. Was this how they were to be repaid? The *Penrith Observer* called the men 'our devoted volunteers' and referred to a meeting to be held by the local men on Saturday 8th July.

Two days prior to the meeting Dan Daley prepared to attend a dance with his wife, Alice, organised by the Gala Committee of the town. Dan had been feeling a little under the weather for some weeks after having been diagnosed with a gastric ulcer, and during the evening, he was taken ill and had to excuse himself from the ball, disappointing for him, and especially Alice, on an all-too-rare- night out.

Struggling through the next couple of days, Dan attended the lively gathering of the Penrith Volunteers on 8th July, at The George Hotel, where some four years earlier they had attended a concert given in their honour the night before they left to hear their call to arms. Now they were here to discuss the cuts in volunteer numbers. Passions ran high among the men and poor Captain Haswell, who had himself joined the Volunteer movement in 1892 and had led the men himself to South Africa, could do little to assuage their anger and disappointment. The meeting broke up unsatisfactorily for the dejected volunteers, and they returned home without having gained any assurances about their future.

Monday 10th July was another regular summer's day. Dan, still not feeling too well, went to work as normal, as did his mother, Jane, leaving Alice and baby John at home. By mid-afternoon, the young joiner was still in a state of general malaise, which caused him to be sent home. By the time he had walked the few hundred paces along Stricklandgate, he was doubled up in agony. His wife and sister, Mary Jane, took him into the house and looked on in abject terror as Dan writhed on the floor with blood frothing from his mouth. One of the women rushed for the doctor but by the time he arrived, Dan Daley was dead: he was 26 years old.

The death certificate stated he died of 'haemoptysis' (This is the expectoration of blood or bloodstained sputum. It is frothy and bright red, and extremely distressing for both patient and for those who witness their agony.) Causes of haemoptysis can vary: a respiratory tract infection or hypertension can be contributing factors. There are others however, that give us clues to Dan's death. A history of asthma and/or bronchitis can put individuals at risk, and although there is no evidence that Dan himself suffered from either, his father clearly did (Daniel senior died in 1881, with both ailments being listed as the cause of death). Another contributing factor is the question of smoking: virtually everyone smoked at this period and there is written evidence that Dan and the volunteers were presented with pipes and cigarettes before during and after their campaign. It is fair to assume therefore that Daley was a regular smoker like most of his contemporaries. The final, and perhaps significant, cause of haemoptysis is a significant weight loss, during a short time period, which could suggest an underlying malignancy. Although Dan had been home for four years, his malarial infection in South Africa caused such weight loss. Could it be that one or all of these factors contributed sufficiently to tragically weaken his constitution? Whatever the cause, it would appear that his gastric ulcer had not only contributed to his demise, but had disastrously masked a more serious problem. There may even be a possibility that a tumour in the stomach was misdiagnosed as an ulcer — the haemoptysis could well have been a result of stomach cancer.

This was not uppermost in the minds of those in the local community, who gathered in shock as news of the popular young lad's passing spread. Both the *Herald* and the *Observer* reported on the tragic news and advised their readers of the funeral, which would take place with full military honours on Thursday 13th July.

Family members and fellow workers, footballers and Foresters, all joined as mourners to pay their respects — a good turn out. At two o'clock,

PTE 7185 Daniel Daly of Penrith
Who Served with the
Volunteer Battalion of
The Border Regiment During
The Boer War. Died 1905

Dan Daley's South Africa campaign medal

Dan's colleagues from the Penrith Volunteers carried the pitch pine coffin, draped with the union flag, out of the house. Captain Haswell and many of Dan's colleagues from South Africa, including Joe Harrison, led the funeral procession as it wound its way up to the cemetery on Beacon Edge, overlooking the town.

Dan's mother, Jane, made arrangements for the young man to be buried in the same grave as his father (who also died relatively young, at 48). The Reverend Father Buckley conducted the service at the florally bedecked graveside and William Patrickson read from the Foresters' service and paid tribute to the young man's work in the community, as his grief-stricken, disbelieving widow was comforted by Jane. The poignant silence that followed was ended with the snapping of a volley of shots over the coffin, provided by a non-active service squad of volunteers. The service was brought to an end with a sole bugler playing The Last Post.

POSTSCRIPT

With the 'winning' of the Boer War in 1902, 167,000 square miles had been added to the British Empire. But paradoxically it also signalled the end of the most dominant empire the world had ever seen, as its legacy was debt and the almost universal denouncement of imperialism. 'We have had an imperial lesson,' wrote Rudyard Kipling, and the Liberal backlash to the war struck a resounding chord with the voting public, the upshot being, in 1906, one of biggest election landslides in British election history. The Union of the four states into one South Africa came in 1910, as 'Empire' continued its inexorable move towards a more politically correct 'Commonwealth.'

Dan Daley's colleagues in the volunteer units survived a certain amount of tinkering with the system until they were completely reorganised and became the Territorial Army in 1908. Some of the men transferred into the T.A. and fought with the Border Regiment in the First World War. Dan's friend and colleague, Joseph Harrison, remained in Penrith for the rest of his life. He was a well-known shoemaker in Burrowgate and was an active organiser of the reunions of the Boer War veterans, up to and including as late as 1949. Two headline stars of the war, General Sir Redvers Buller and Lord Baden-Powell, actually visited Penrith some years later to give a talk on education and to inspect the local Boy Scouts respectively. (Baden-Powell formed the Boy Scout movement in 1908.)

One of the purposes of this book is to give the likes of Dan Daley and Joe Harrison parity with the likes of Roberts and Baden-Powell. That said, this volume has, without doubt, concentrated mainly on the adventures and exploits of men, whether ordinary or extraordinary. If it is a truism therefore, that behind every great man is a great woman, then clearly there is an imbalance and the likes of Jane Daley (nee Sanderson) deserve special mention.

The concept of the little Victorian woman whose place was in the home was developed through the writings of Hannah More (1745-1833). 'Men are formed for the more public exhibitions on the great theatre of human life, whilst women are best suited to the smaller scale of the domestic,' she argued towards the end of her life. 'Men prefer their wives to be meek and virtuous. Wives should find their fulfilment through service to others through the exercise of moral influence.' This may have sat well in a Jane Austen novel, but for thousands of working class women in Victorian and

Edwardian Britain, life was riddled with hardship and injustice.

Most women worked through necessity rather than choice and many others looked forward to marriage as a release from poverty and uncertainty. This is possibly the expedient used by Jane Sanderson to escape her early existence. She was born in the St Andrew's Workhouse, Penrith, on 1st November 1837, to her unmarried, illiterate mother, Ann. Raised in such austere surroundings, she was joined by her brother William, born nine years later (possibly to a different father). Jane married Daniel Daley in 1862, a marriage that produced five children before his untimely death in 1881. This was Jane's life: pauper and housekeeper, wife and widow, mother and worker, grandmother, godmother and guardian, before experiencing the unimaginable heartbreak of a mother outliving her child, when her youngest, Dan, died suddenly in 1905. Jane herself passed away on 5th October 1908, aged 70.

I am left concluding that if ordinary men receive little recognition for their efforts, then ordinary women receive even less for theirs. Jane's immediate (and extended) family continued to live in Penrith into the 1950s.

PRINCIPAL SOURCES

Books

Bardgett, Colin	*The Black Angel*	(Bookcase, 1995)
Blake, Joyce & Brian	*The Story of Carlisle*	(Carlisle Ed Comm, 1958)
Blake, RLV French	*The 17th/21st Lancers 1759-1993*	(Leo Cooper Ltd, 1993)
Bouch, CML & Jones, GP	*The Lake Counties 1500-1830*	(Manchester Unv Press, 1968)
David, Saul	*The Indian Mutiny 1857*	(Penguin Viking, 2002)
Davies, Norman	*The Isles, A History*	(Macmillan, 1999)
Eden District Council	*Penrith - A Historical Record in Photographs*	(Eden District Council, 2000)
Farish, William	*The Struggles of a Hand-Loom Weaver*	(Caliban Books, 1996)
Farwell, Byron	*The Great Boer War*	(Wordsworth Ed Ltd, 1999)
Fortescue, Hon JW	*The History of the 17th Lancers*	(Macmillan & Co, 1895)
Furness, William	*History of Penrith*	(William Furness, 1894)
Harvey, Basil	*The Rifle Brigade*	(Leo Cooper Ltd, 1975)
Hurst, John	*The Blues - A History of Penrith Football Club*	(Penrith Football Club, 1994)
Kerr, Paul	*The Crimean War*	(Boxtree, 1997)
Perriam, DR	*Carlisle, An Illustrated History*	(Bookcase, 1992)
Rawlinson, Robert	*Carlisle Sanitary Conditions*	(HM Stationary Office, 1850)
Rollinson, William	*The History of Cumberland and Westmorland*	(Phillimore & Co, 1978)
Schama, Simon	*A History of Britain Vol II*	(BBC Worldwide Ltd, 2001)
Schama, Simon	*A History of Britain Vol III*	(BBC Worldwide, Ltd, 2002)

Shepherd, Margaret E	*From Hellgill to Bridge End*	(Unv Herfordshire Press 2003)
Stanley, Peter	*The White Mutiny*	(Hurst & Co. 1998)
Sutherland, Douglas	*Tried and Valliant*	(Lee Cooper Ltd, 1972)
Towill, Sydney	*Carlisle*	(Carnegie Publishing, 1991)
Towill, Sydney	*Georgian and Victorian Carlisle*	(Carnegie Publishing, 1996)
Wood, Sir Evelyn V.C.	*From Midshipman to Field Marshall*	(Methuen & Co, 1906)

Articles & Public Reports

Armstrong, WA	*Trends of Mortality in Cumberland between 1780-1840*	1981
Barnes, J	*Thesis on Popular Protest and Radical Politics 1790-1850*	1981
Rawlinson, R	*Report to General Board of Health on City of Carlisle*	1850
Rawlinson, R	*Report to General Board of Health on parish of Penrith*	1849
Reid, DB	*Report on Sanitary State of Carlisle*	1845

Newspapers & Magazines

Files of the *Carlisle Examiner*
Files of the *Carlisle Journal*
Files of the *Carlisle Patriot*
Files of the *Daily Telegraph*
Files of the *Mid Cumberland & North Westmorland Herald*
Files of the *Penrith Herald*
Files of the *Penrith Observer*
Files of *The Times*
The *Regiment Magazine*, Issue Twenty

Records & Private Papers

Church Records of All Saints Church, Cockermouth 1790-1840
Church Records of St Andrew's Church, Penrith 1850-1880
Church Records of St Catherine's Church, Penrith 1830-1910
Church Records of St Mary's, Carlisle 1800-1900
Diary of Frank Scott, 1900-1920
Papers belonging to the Border and King's Own Royal Border Regiment (including the regimental diaries from the Boer War)
Papers belonging to the Queen's Royal Lancers (including Sergeant Wightman's diary of the Central India campaign)
School Log - St Catherine's School, Penrith 1876-1907
Service Records of Private Dan Daley (Public Records Office)
Service Records of Private Isaac Scott (Public Records Office)
Service Records of Private Jacob Reed (Public Records Office)

Web sites

BBC History
Carlisle History
Channel4 History
Cumbria Industries
Genuki
National Army Museum
The Anglo-Boer War Museum
The Crimean War Research Society
The History of Regiments in the British Army
The Imperial War Museum
The War Times Journal

INDEX

A

B

Other books by Martin Daley:

GLORY BOY!

SHERLOCK HOLMES AND THE CARLISLE
ADVENTURE OF THE SPANISH DRUMS

THE CARLISLE FLOODS: ONE STORY